MW00416959

The Econometrics of
Corporate Governance
Studies

The Econometrics of Corporate Governance Studies

Sanjai Bhagat and
Richard H. Jefferis, Jr.

The MIT Press
Cambridge, Massachusetts
London, England

This book was set in Palatino by Asco Typesetters, Hong Kong. Printed and bound in the United States of America.

Library of Congress Cataloging-in-Publication Data

Bhagat, Sanjai.
  The econometrics of corporate governance studies / Sanjai Bhagat and Richard H. Jefferis, Jr.
    p. cm.
  Includes bibliographical references and index.
  ISBN 0-262-02517-5 (hc. : alk. paper)
  1. Corporate governance—Econometrics models. I. Jefferis, Richard H. II. Title.
HD2741 .B48 2002
658.4—dc21   2001056203

To the loving memory of our parents
Bernice
Usha
Mahendra
Richard

Contents

Preface

A vast theoretical and empirical literature in corporate finance considers the interrelationships between corporate governance, takeovers, management turnover, corporate performance, corporate capital structure, and corporate ownership structure. Most of the extant literature considers the relationship between two of these variables at a time—for example, the relationship between ownership and performance or the relationship between corporate governance and takeovers. *We argue that takeover defenses, takeovers, management turnover, corporate performance, capital structure, and corporate ownership structure are interrelated. Hence, from an econometric viewpoint, the proper way to study the relationship between any two of these variables would be to set up a system of simultaneous equations that specifies the relationships between these six variables. However, specification and estimation of such a system of simultaneous equations are nontrivial.* To illustrate this problem in a meaningful manner, we consider the following two questions that have received considerable attention in the literature and have significant policy implications: (1) do antitakeover measures prevent takeovers, and (2) do antitakeover measures help managers enhance their job tenure?

Publicly held corporations often adopt antitakeover measures that make a company takeover that is opposed by that company's management more difficult (and sometimes impossible). More often than not, a management-opposed takeover results in the departure of these managers from the target company. Hence, antitakeover measures, while ostensibly intended to prevent management-opposed takeovers, may also aid the managers of the particular company in increasing (the security of) their job tenure. During the past two decades an overwhelming majority of publicly held U.S. corporations have adopted such antitakeover measures.

In this book, we examine the impact of firm performance, owner-ship structure, and corporate takeover defenses on takeover activ-ity and managerial turnover. Our focus is the efficacy of corporate takeover defense. The literature suggests that takeovers and the managerial labor market serve to discipline poor performers in the managerial ranks and also suggests that corporate takeover defenses are designed to shield incumbent managers from these forces. If this is in fact the case, and the belief that motivates the adoption of takeover defenses is rational, the presence of these defenses should be associated with a decline in takeover activity and extended job tenure for managers.

The results presented here provide little support for this hypothe-sis. We find that antitakeover measures are not effective in prevent-ing takeovers, nor are they effective in enhancing management's job tenure. We do observe a negative correlation between takeover activ-ity and takeover defense that is statistically significant. However, when we control for the financial performance of the company, we do not observe the negative relation between takeover activity and takeover defense. In a model that allows the relationship between performance and takeover activity to vary with takeover defense, we find that defensive activity is ineffective.

In the case of management turnover, our results are even stronger. The frequency of CEO departures is uncorrelated with the status of takeover defenses at firms in our sample. This statement is consistent with both simple correlations and with the estimates from probit models, where we find that turnover is related to performance. At firms with poison pill defenses, there is a statistically significant relationship between management turnover and performance.

We stress that these results do not imply that defensive activity is costless to shareholders. It may well be the case that managers who are shielded by takeover defenses perform less well than they would have had the takeover defenses not been in place. This hypothesis is consistent with both the results reported here and with indirect evidence from announcement returns. Our evidence does, however, suggest quite strongly that takeover defenses are not completely effective in insulating managers from the consequences of poor cor-porate financial performance.

Acknowledgments

We thank workshop participants at the American Finance Association and the Western Finance Association meetings, Arizona State University, George Mason Law School, University of Illinois (Champaign), University of Pittsburgh, Princeton University, Southern Methodist University, University of Virginia, the U.S. Securities and Exchange Commission, and Vanderbilt University for their helpful comments on earlier drafts of chapters 5 and 6 of this monograph. We thank the College of Business Research Committee at the University of Colorado for partial financial support for this research. We also thank Elizabeth Murry and Victoria Richardson Warneck of MIT Press for their constant encouragement in getting us to complete this book.

1   Introduction

1.1 Historical Perspective

Corporate managers are the dominant power brokers in large, U.S. corporations. Roe (1994) notes that our particular political and economic history might be responsible for the dominance of corporate managers. A substantial literature going back to Berle and Means (1932) has noted the relative lack of accountability of corporate managers and argued that corporate performance in the United States would be improved if corporations had monitors to oversee the managers (see Jensen and Meckling 1976). After World War II through the early 1970s, the United States was the dominant economic power in the world. This economic dominance in this period is consistent with the argument that the corporate governance and power structure that had evolved here was appropriate for the United States— that is, corporate America was delivering the goods. Hence, there was no need to reconsider the corporate power structure. Others might argue that U.S. global economic dominance in this period was a direct result of the war, which had destroyed the physical and economic infrastructure of most other major economic players in the world.

By the late 1970s, it seemed evident to even casual observers of the economy that U.S. corporations were losing their global competitive edge. Observers in the popular media argued that the decline in our global competitiveness was due to mismanagement of corporate resources by corporate managers. The argument went that corporate managers were more interested in increasing and managing their empires; serving the shareholders' interest was of secondary importance. These observers noted that the reason managers were successful in engaging in such behavior was lack of meaningful oversight of their decisions and lack of an alternate power with disciplining authority.

In the 1980s, hostile bidders (raiders) perhaps served this monitoring or disciplining role. However, concerns about the role of such raiders on the long-term impact on corporations and about the near-term impact on other stakeholders were raised (see Bhagat, Shleifer, and Vishny 1990). At some point in the late 1980s, hostile takeovers became much rarer; Comment and Schwert (1995) provide a discussion and potential explanations of this. Starting in the early 1990s, both the popular and academic commentators started emphasizing the monitoring role of "relational investors" (see Bhagat, Black, and Blair 2001).

1.2   Corporate Antitakeover Devices

Some have suggested that corporate antitakeover devices (such as antitakeover amendments and poison pills) played a role in diminishing the occurrence of takeovers in the late 1980s. Antitakeover amendments are proposed by corporate boards and approved by shareholders; these amendments amend the corporate charter to make control of the corporation more difficult without the existing board's approval. A classified board amendment provides for the election of typically a third of the board in any annual election; this extends the time required to elect a majority in the board. A fair-price provision may require that all shareholders be paid the same price that any potential acquirer paid for any shares during a certain period. Some corporations have amended their charter to reincorporate in Delaware—a state that is generally considered to be manager-friendly. Poison pills are typically adopted without shareholder approval. While poison pills come in many flavors, they typically impose a very high cost on a potential acquirer that is disapproved of by the board. For example, the pill may require the acquirer to assume large financial liabilities, dilute the acquirer's equity, or lessen the voting power of the acquirer's equity. Brickley, Lease, and Smith (1988) and Bruner (1991) offer descriptions of these antitakeover provisions.

1.3   The Econometric Problem of Measuring the Impact of Antitakeover Provisions

The theoretical and empirical literature in corporate finance considers the interrelationships between corporate governance, takeovers, management turnover, corporate performance, corporate capital structure, and corporate ownership structure. Most of the extant literature considers the relationship between two of these variables at a time—for example, the relationship between ownership and performance or the relationship between corporate governance and takeovers.

The following is a sampling from the above-mentioned literature: Pound (1987) and Comment and Schwert (1995) consider the effect of takeover defenses on takeover activity; Morck, Shleifer, and Vishny (1989) examine the effect of corporate ownership and firm performance on takeover activity and management turnover; DeAngelo and DeAngelo (1989), Martin and McConnell (1991), Denis and Serrano (1996), and Mikkelson and Partch (1997) consider the effect of firm performance on management turnover; Denis, Denis, and Sarin (1997) consider the effect of ownership structure on management turnover; Bhagat and Jefferis (1991) consider the impact of corporate ownership structure on takeover defenses; Ikenberry and Lakonishok (1993) investigate the effect of firm performance on takeover activity; Berkovitch, Israel, and Spiegel (1998) examine the impact of capital structure on management compensation; Mahrt-Smith (2000) studies the relationship between ownership and capital structure; Garvey and Hanka (1999) investigate the impact of corporate governance on capital structure; McConnell and Servaes (1990), Hermalin and Weisbach (1991), Loderer and Martin (1997), Cho (1998), Himmelberg, Hubbard, and Palia (1999), and Demsetz and Villalonga (2001) study the relationship between ownership structure and corporate performance; and DeAngelo and DeAngelo (2000) and Fenn and Liang (2001) focus on ownership structure and the corporate payout policy.

We argue that takeover defenses, takeovers, management turnover, corporate performance, capital structure, and corporate ownership structure are interrelated. Hence, from an econometric viewpoint, the proper way to study the relationship between any two of these variables would be to set up a system of simultaneous equations that specifies the relationships between these six variables. However, specification and estimation of such a system of simultaneous equations are nontrivial.

For example, econometric models that acknowledge the possibility that performance, ownership, and takeover defenses influence takeovers do not necessarily yield consistent estimates for the parameters of interest. Identification requires some combination of exclusion restrictions, assumptions about the joint distribution of the error terms, and restrictions on the functional form of the structural equations. Maddala (1983) discusses restrictions that identify the model when the error terms are normally distributed. Identification in *single-equation* semiparametric index models—where the functional form is unknown and the explanatory variables in that equation are continuous, known functions of a basic parameter vector—is discussed by Ichimura and Lee (1991). Estimation of a system of equations in the absence of strong restrictions on *both* the functional form of the equations and the joint distribution of error terms is, to the best of our knowledge, an unsolved problem.

We are unaware of a model of takeover defense that implies specific functional forms. If these functions are linear, identification may be attained through either strong distributional assumptions or exclusion restrictions. Maddala (1983) and Amemiya (1985) discuss restrictions on the error terms that identify the model in the absence of exclusion restrictions. But these restrictions are inconsistent with incentive-based explanations of takeover defense, since unobservable characteristics of managerial behavior or type will be reflected in all of the error terms. Exclusion restrictions are therefore the most likely path to identification.

The hypothesis that we wish to test—that takeover defense affects the likelihood of takeover activity—suggests that exclusion restrictions would be difficult to justify. Intuitively, variables that affect the likelihood of a takeover will be reflected in the structure of takeover defenses.

To illustrate the above-mentioned econometric problems in a meaningful manner, we consider the following two questions: (1) do antitakeover measures prevent takeovers, and (2) do antitakeover measures help managers enhance their job tenure?

We examine the impact of firm performance, ownership structure, and corporate governance (which includes corporate antitakeover devices) on takeover activity and managerial turnover. Our focus is the impact of corporate takeover defense on the relationship between performance and takeover activity and the impact of corporate takeover defense on the relationship between performance and managerial turnover.

The literature suggests that takeovers and the managerial labor market discipline poor performers in the managerial ranks and also suggests that takeover defenses are proposed by incumbent managers to shield themselves from these forces; Jarrell, Brickley, and Netter

(1988) summarize this literature.[1] DeAngelo and Rice (1983) characterize such self-serving behavior as the managerial entrenchment hypothesis.

An alternative interpretation of corporate takeover defenses is that they represent an agreement that alters the distribution of bargaining power among managers, shareholders, the board of directors, and outsiders but not necessarily in a manner that favors managers. Specifically, such takeover defenses may provide managers with additional incentives to invest in firm-specific human capital and to negotiate a higher bid premium in a takeover; DeAngelo and Rice (1983) characterize this as the shareholder interests hypothesis. Knoeber (1986) points to a "fundamental paradox" between these two hypotheses: he notes that proponents of the managerial entrenchment hypothesis oppose takeover defenses since they inhibit takeovers that are a voluntary transaction between target and bidder shareholders. Knoeber argues that takeover defenses are also a voluntary transaction among target shareholders, board of directors, and managers. A manager who is shielded by takeover defenses must still answer to a board of directors; both management and the board may be vulnerable to pressure from quarters other than the direct threat of a hostile takeover. The recent experience of American Express, IBM, and General Motors illustrates this point

By contrasting the relationship between performance and takeovers (or managerial turnover) at firms that have takeover defenses with the relationship between performance and takeovers (or managerial turnover) at firms that do not have takeover defenses, we seek to learn whether defensive activity does in fact insulate managers from market discipline. The evidence from this investigation complements the indirect evidence from announcement returns.

Our effort builds on the work of Palepu (1986), Morck, Shleifer, and Vishny (1989), Martin and McConnell (1991), Denis and Serrano (1996), and Mikkelson and Partch (1997), who document poor financial performance prior to takeovers. We incorporate their insights into a model that also acknowledges the potential influence of take-

---

1. Bhagat and Jefferis (1991) document negative announcement returns for antitakeover amendments approved by shareholders and reconcile their results with ambiguous evidence from earlier studies. Ryngaert (1988) provides evidence concerning the impact of poison pills on shareholder wealth. Poison pills are usually adopted by the board without being submitted to shareholders for approval and are associated with a statistically significant decline in shareholder wealth.

over defenses and ownership on control activity. We contribute to the growing literature on the effect of corporate governance on firm performance: Bhagat, Carey, and Elson (1999), Bhagat and Black (2001), and Core, Holthausen, and Larcker (1999). Our work emphasizes the endogeneity in the relationship among governance, ownership, performance, and compensation. We also contribute to the literature on the effect of corporate performance on management turnover: Warner, Watts, and Wruck (1988), Weisbach (1988), and Denis and Denis (1995).[2]

We control for the influence of ownership and takeover defense in evaluating the effect of performance on turnover.[3] Finally, our econometric approach and our examination of managerial turnover as well as takeover activity distinguish our work from Pound (1987), who reports that takeover defenses are associated with a decline in the frequency of takeover activity.

The distinction between our work and that of earlier authors is significant. We show that the inference that takeover defenses decrease the frequency of takeover activity, which is consistent with the correlations reported by Pound, is spurious and attributable to the omission of performance from the econometric model. We also demonstrate that the omission of takeover defenses from a model of the relationship between takeovers (or management turnover) and performance results in a specification error that biases inference about the influence of performance on takeover activity (or management turnover). Finally, our results suggest that self-selection plays an important role in models that relate takeover defenses to performance.

We base our analysis on the experience of a choice-based sample of firms during the years 1984 through 1987. This sample has two distinctive features. First, the array of takeover defenses in place at sample firms during this time period varies widely, ranging from no defense to a combination of classified board provisions, poison pills, and fair-price amendments. *This variation, which enhances the statistical power of our analysis, would deteriorate if we considered a later time*

---

2. Though the results of these papers are consistent with the managerial labor market disciplining poor performance, Jensen and Murphy (1990) note that the expected costs of dismissals on managers of poorly performing firms are economically small.

3. We consider the effect of capital structure indirectly through its effect on ownership structure. A growing recent literature considers the relationship among capital structure, ownership structure, and managerial compensation. The concerns regarding the endogeneity among these relationships as noted in this book would apply to these papers.

period when a larger fraction of firms had adopted takeover defenses, especially poison pills. The time frame is also significant because it precedes the advent of restrictive state antitakeover statutes. A cross-sectional analysis based on data from a later period would reflect the presence of these state statutes; the rapid proliferation of state antitakeover statutes after 1987 and the concentration of incorporations in Delaware would make it difficult to maintain statistical power while controlling for the influence of state law.

Comment and Schwert (1995) discuss the timing of corporate antitakeover defenses and state antitakeover statutes. They plot the percentage of firms that were listed on the New York Stock Exchange and America Stock Exchange and that were covered by state antitakeover statutes from 1975 through 1991. Prior to 1986, fewer than 5 percent of the firms were covered by such state antitakeover statutes; by 1987, about 15 percent of the firms were covered, and by 1988, about 70 percent of the firms were covered by these statutes. Danielson and Karpoff (1998) document similar evidence.

We find that the joint distribution of takeover activity and takeover defense and the joint distribution of management turnover and takeover defense are consistent with the hypothesis that takeover defenses insulate managers from the discipline of the takeover market. In our sample, the frequency of takeovers at firms that have takeover defenses is much lower than the frequency of takeovers at firms that do not have defenses. This result is consistent with the findings of Pound. We also find evidence of a strong negative relationship between takeover defense and the complete turnover of top management.

An examination of financial performance suggests that it would be inappropriate to deduce from these correlations that takeover defenses attenuate the link between performance and discipline. We compare the performance of firms that experience takeovers to the performance of firms that do not experience a struggle for control and find that in the period preceding the adoption of takeover defenses, firms not involved in takeovers outperform those that are involved in subsequent takeover activity. Similar results obtain in the case of managerial turnover. These relationships, which are consistent with a disciplinary role for takeovers and management turnover, hold for both the entire sample (which includes firms without takeover defenses) and for firms that have takeover defenses. We also observe a significant relationship between ownership structure and both takeover activity and managerial turnover.

Our observations about ownership and performance motivate a cross-sectional examination of the relationship between takeover activity and takeover defense and the relationship between managerial turnover and takeover defense. Estimates from probit models indicate that performance swamps the influence of all other factors, including takeover defenses, in explaining the experience of firms with respect to managerial turnover and takeover activity. The interpretation of our results is clouded by a concern about econometric identification and specification diagnostics from the probit model. But our analysis suggests quite strongly that takeover activity and managerial turnover are linked to performance, even at firms that have takeover defenses. In the data examined here, firm performance is more important than takeover defense in explaining the frequency of takeover activity and managerial turnover.

1.4   State Antitakeover Statutes

The focus of this book is on corporate antitakeover defenses that are implemented by corporate boards (sometimes subject to shareholder approval). These corporate antitakeover defenses are distinct from state antitakeover statutes, though both attempt to make corporate takeovers more difficult.

Prior to 1982, few states had any antitakeover statute. From 1982 through 1990, 35 states enacted over 70 antitakeover statutes; the jurisdiction of these states covers about 90 percent of publicly listed U.S. corporations. Some of these statutes include stakeholder provisions that authorize corporate directors to consider the impact of a potential takeover on all corporate stakeholders, such as employees, customers, suppliers, and not just shareholders. The statutes also include control share provisions that remove the voting right of a large block shareholder (typically, a 20 percent blockholder) until a majority of all disinterested shareholders vote to restore these voting rights and labor contracts provisions that prevent firms from terminating existing labor contracts subsequent to a takeover. Karpoff and Malatesta (1989) and Wahal, Wiles, and Zenner (1995) describe and analyze these state antitakeover statutes. These and other authors document a negative impact on shareholders of affected corporations of such statutes. These studies do not explicitly consider the impact of such statutes on takeover activity.

2   Econometrics of Corporate Governance Studies

2.1   Corporate Control, Performance, Governance, and Ownership Structure

As noted earlier, an extensive theoretical and empirical literature in corporate finance considers the interrelationships between corporate governance, takeovers, management turnover, corporate performance, corporate capital structure, and corporate ownership structure. In section 2.1, we review the theoretical and empirical literature that provides support for relationships among subsets of these variables.

2.1.1   Corporate Control, Performance, and Governance

The interpretation of takeovers and managerial turnover as mechanisms for discipline may be motivated by incentive-based economic models of managerial behavior. Broadly speaking, these models fall into two categories. In agency models, a divergence in the interests of managers and shareholders causes managers to take actions that are costly to shareholders. Contracts cannot preclude this activity if shareholders are unable to observe managerial behavior directly, but ownership by the manager may be used to induce managers to act in a manner that is consistent with the interest of shareholders.[1]

---

1. This suggests a positive relationship between ownership and performance. However, as pointed out by Stulz (1988), ownership has both an incentive effect through a stake in the firm's cash flows and an entrenchment effect through control of votes. As ownership gets large enough, there is no way to take a corporation over. Recent evidence in Himmelberg, Hubbard, and Palia (1999) suggests that econometric estimation of the effect of managerial ownership may be quite difficult for the reasons noted later in this chapter.

Performance is reflected in managerial payoffs, which may be interpreted as including takeovers and managerial turnover. Grossman and Hart (1983) describe this problem.

Adverse-selection models are motivated by the hypothesis of differential ability that cannot be observed by shareholders. In this setting, ownership may be used to induce revelation of the manager's private information about cash flow or his ability to generate cash flow, which cannot be observed directly by shareholders. Performance provides information to the principal about the ability of the manager and is therefore reflected in managerial payoffs, which may include dismissal for poor performance. A general treatment is provided by Myerson (1987).

In this setting, takeover defenses may be interpreted as a characteristic of the contract that governs relations between shareholders and managers. This interpretation is clearly warranted in the case of charter amendments that are enacted through a shareholder vote. With poison pills and other defenses that are adopted unilaterally, the interpretation of takeover defenses as contract provisions may be problematical. But in either case, the presence of takeover defenses is affected by the same unobservable features of managerial behavior or ability that are linked to ownership and performance.

2.1.2 Corporate Governance and Performance

Most large American public companies have boards with a majority of independent directors; almost all have a majority of outside directors. This pattern reflects the common view that the board's principal task is to monitor management and that only independent directors can be vigorous monitors. In contrast, an insider-dominated board is seen as a device for management entrenchment (for example, Millstein 1993; American Law Institute 1994). The proposition that large-company boards should consist mostly of independent directors has become conventional wisdom. For example, guidelines adopted by the Council of Institutional Investors (1998) call for at least two-thirds of a company's directors to be independent; guidelines adopted by the California Public Employees Retirement System (1998) and by the National Association of Corporate Directors (1996) call for boards to have a "substantial majority" of independent directors. This conventional wisdom has only an occasional dissenting voice (for example, Longstreth 1994).

Prior studies of the effect of board composition on firm performance generally adopt one of two approaches. The first approach involves studying how board composition affects the board's behavior on discrete tasks, such as replacing the CEO, awarding golden parachutes, or making or defending against a takeover bid. This approach can involve tractable data, which makes it easier for researchers to find statistically significant results. But it doesn't tell us how board composition affects overall firm performance. For example, there is evidence that firms with majority-independent boards perform better on particular tasks, such as replacing the CEO (Weisbach 1988) and making takeover bids (Byrd and Hickman 1992). But these firms could perform worse on other tasks that cannot readily be studied using this approach (such as appointing a new CEO or choosing a new strategic direction for the firm), leading to no net advantage in overall performance. Rosenstein and Wyatt (1990) find that stock prices increase by about 0.2 percent, on average, when companies appoint additional outside directors. This increase, while statistically significant, is economically small and could reflect signaling effects. Appointing an additional independent director could signal that a company plans to address its business problems, even if board composition doesn't affect the company's ability to address these problems. Rosenstein and Wyatt (1997) find that stock prices neither increase nor decrease on average when an *insider* is added to the board.

Bhagat and Black (2001) adopt the second approach of examining directly the correlation between board composition and firm performance. This approach allows us to examine the "bottom line" of firm performance (unlike the first approach) but involves much less tractable data. Firm performance must be measured over a long period, which means that performance measures are noisy and perhaps misspecified; this is discussed in section 2.1.3.2.

Prior research does not establish a clear correlation between board independence and firm performance. Baysinger and Butler (1985), Hermalin and Weisbach (1991), and MacAvoy, Cantor, Dana, and Peck (1983) all report no significant same-year correlation between board composition and various measures of corporate performance. Baysinger and Butler report that the proportion of independent directors in 1970 correlates with *1980* industry-adjusted return on equity. However, their 10-year lag period is rather long for any effects of board composition on performance to persist.

Three recent studies offer hints that firms with a high percentage of independent directors may perform *worse*. Yermack (1996) reports a significant negative correlation between proportion of independent directors and contemporaneous Tobin's q but no significant correlation for several other performance variables—sales per assets, operating income per assets, or operating income per sales. Agrawal and Knoeber (1996) report a negative correlation between proportion of outside directors and Tobin's q. Klein (1998) reports a significant negative correlation between a measure of change in market value of equity and proportion of independent directors but insignificant results for return on assets and raw stock-market returns.

Board composition could affect firm performance, but firm performance could also affect the firm's future board composition. The factors that determine board composition are not well understood, but board composition is known to be related to industry (Agrawal and Knoeber 1999) and to a firm's ownership structure (firms with high inside ownership have less independent boards) (see Bhagat and Black 2001). If board composition is endogenous, ordinary least squares (OLS) coefficient estimates can be biased. Simultaneous equations methods can address endogeneity but are often more sensitive than OLS to model misspecification (see Barnhart and Rosenstein 1998).

Several researchers have examined whether board composition is endogenously related to firm performance, with inconsistent results. Hermalin and Weisbach (1988) and Weisbach (1988) report that the proportion of independent directors on large-firm boards increases slightly when a company has performed poorly: firms in the bottom performance decile in year X increase their proportion of independent directors by around 1 percent in year $X + 1$, relative to other firms, from 1972 through 1983. In contrast, Klein (1998) finds no tendency for firms in the bottom quintile for 1991 stock-price returns to add more independent directors in 1992 and 1993 than firms in the top quintile. Denis and Sarin (1999) report that firms that substantially increase their proportion of independent directors had *above-average* stock-price returns in the previous year. They also report that average board composition for a group of firms changes slowly over time and that board composition tends to regress to the mean, with firms with a high (low) proportion of independent directors reducing (increasing) this percentage over time.

Bhagat and Black (2001) address the possible endogeneity of board independence and firm performance by adopting a three-stage least squares (3SLS) approach, as described in Theil (1971); this permits firm performance, board independence, and CEO ownership to be endogenously determined. 3SLS is a systems estimating procedure that estimates all the identified structural equations together as a set, instead of estimating the structural parameters of each equation separately as is the case with the two-stage least squares (2SLS) procedure. The 3SLS is a full-information method because it utilizes knowledge of all the restrictions in the entire system when estimating the structural parameters. The 3SLS estimator is consistent and in general is asymptotically more efficient than the 2SLS estimator (see Mikhail 1975).

Bhagat and Black (2001) find a reasonably strong correlation between poor performance and subsequent increase in board independence. The change in board independence seems to be driven by poor performance rather than by firm and industry growth opportunities. However, there is no evidence that greater board independence leads to improved firm performance.

2.1.3 Corporate Ownership and Performance

The corporate form has consistently proven to be a superior method of business organization. Great industrial economies have grown and prospered where the corporate legal structure has been prevalent. This organizational form, however, has not existed and served without flaw. The multiple problems arising out of the fundamental agency nature of the corporate relationship have continually hindered its complete economic effectiveness. Where ownership and management are structurally separated, how does one ensure effective operational efficiencies? In the late nineteenth century, the solution lay in the establishment of a powerful monitoring intermediary—the board of directors, whose primary responsibility was management oversight and control for the benefit of the residual equity owners. To ensure an effective agency, the board was chosen by and comprised generally of the business's largest shareholders. Substantial shareholdership acted to align board and shareholder interests to create the best incentive for effective oversight. Additionally, legal fiduciary duties evolved to prevent director self dealing, through the medium of the duty of loyalty, and to discourage lax monitoring, through the duty of care. No direct compensation for board service was permitted. By the early 1930s, however, in the largest public corporations, the board was no longer essentially the dominion of the company's most substantial shareholders.

The early twentieth century witnessed not only the phenomenal growth of the American economy but also the growth of those corporate entities whose activities comprised that economy. Corporations were no longer local ventures owned, controlled, and managed by a handful of local entrepreneurs but instead had become national in size and scope. Concomitant with the rise of the large-scale corporation came the development of the professional management class, whose skills were needed to run such far-flung enterprises. And as the capitalization required to maintain such entities grew, so did the number of individuals required to contribute the funds to create such capital. Thus, we saw the rise of the large-scale public corporation— owned not by a few but by literally thousands and thousands of investors located throughout the nation. And with this growth in the size and ownership levels of the modern corporation, individual shareholdings in these ventures became proportionally smaller and smaller, with no shareholder or shareholding group owning enough stock to dominate the entity. Consequently, the professional managers moved in to fill this control vacuum. Through control of the proxy process, incumbent management nominated its own candidates for board membership. The board of directors, theoretically composed of the representatives of various shareholding groups, instead was comprised of individuals selected by management. The directors' connection with the enterprise generally resulted from a prior relationship with management, not with the stockholding owners, and they often had little or no shareholding stake in the company.

Berle and Means (1932), in their path-breaking book *The Modern Corporation and Private Property*, described this phenomenon of the domination of the large public corporation by professional management as the separation of ownership and control. In such companies, the firm's nominal owners, the shareholders, exercised virtually no control over either day-to-day operations or long-term policy. Instead control was vested in the professional managers, who typically owned only a very small portion of the firm's shares.

One consequence of this phenomenon identified by Berle and Means was the filling of board seats with individuals selected not because they were from the shareholding ranks but because they held some prior relationship with management. Boards were now comprised either of the managers themselves (the *inside directors*) or of associates of the managers who were not otherwise employed by or affiliated with the enterprise (the *outside* or *nonmanagement directors*). This new breed of outside director often had little or no shareholding interest in the enterprise and, as such, no longer represented their own personal financial stakes or those of the other shareholders in rendering board service. However, as the shareholders' legal fiduciaries, the outside directors were still expected to expend independent time and effort in their roles, and, consequently, it began to be recognized that they must now be compensated directly for their activities.

The consequences of this shift in the composition of the board was to exacerbate the agency problem inherent in the corporate form. Without the direct economic incentive of substantial stock ownership, directors, given a natural loyalty to their appointing party and the substantial reputation enhancement and monetary compensation board service came to entail, had little incentive other than their legal fiduciary duties to engage in active managerial oversight. It may also be argued that the large compensation received for board service may have actually acted as a disincentive for active management monitoring, given management control over the director appointment and retention process.

Since the identification of this phenomenon, both legal and finance theorists have struggled to formulate effective solutions. Numerous legal reforms have been proposed, often involving such acts as the creation of the professional "independent director," the development of strengthened board fiduciary duties, or the stimulation of effective institutional shareholder activism. All, it seems, have proven ineffective, as the passive board still flourishes. Shareholders, mindful of disasters at General Motors, IBM, AT&T, Archer-Daniels-Midland, W. R. Grace, and Morrison Knudsen, are keenly aware of this problem. Yet the solution may be simple and obvious. Traditionally, directors, as large shareholders, had a powerful personal incentive to exercise effective oversight. It was the equity ownership that created an effective agency. To recreate this powerful monitoring incentive, directors must become substantial shareholders once again. This is the theoretical underpinning behind the current movement toward equity-based compensation for corporate directors. The idea is to reunite ownership and control through meaningful director stock ownership and hence better management monitoring. Underpinning this theory, however, is the assumption that equity ownership by directors does in fact create more active monitoring. Bhagat, Carey, and Elson (1999) study the link between significant outside director stock ownership, effective monitoring, and firm performance.

The primary responsibility of the corporate board of directors is to engage, monitor, and, when necessary, replace company management. The central criticism of many modern public company boards has been their failure to engage in the kind of active management oversight that results in more effective corporate performance. It has been suggested that substantial equity ownership by the outside directors creates a personal incentive to monitor. An integral part of the monitoring process is the replacement of the CEO when circumstances warrant. An active, nonmanagement-obligated board will presumably make the necessary change sooner rather than later, as a poorly performing management team creates more harm to the overall enterprise the longer it is in place. On the other hand, a management-dominated board, because of its loyalty to the company executives, will take much longer to replace a poorly performing management team because of strong loyalty ties. Consequently, it may be argued that companies where the CEO is replaced expeditiously in times of poor performance may have more active and effective monitoring boards than those companies where ineffective CEO remain in office for longer periods of time. Bhagat, Carey, and Elson (1999) find that when directors owned a greater dollar amount of stock, they were more likely to replace the CEO of a company performing poorly.

2.1.3.1 Endogeneity of Ownership and Performance The above discussion focuses on the costs of diffused share ownership—that is, the impact of ownership structure on performance. Demsetz (1983) argues that since we observe many successful public companies with diffused share ownership, clearly there must be offsetting benefits— for example, better risk bearing. Sometimes, as in the case of leveraged buyouts, when the benefits are substantially less than the costs of diffused share ownership, we do observe that companies undergo rapid and drastic changes in their ownership structure. In other words, ownership structure may be endogenous.

Also, for reasons related to performance-based compensation and insider information, firm performance could be a determinant of ownership. For example, superior firm performance leads to an increase in the value of stock options owned by management, which, if exercised, would increase their share ownership. Also, if there are serious divergences between insider and market expectations of future firm performance, then insiders have an incentive to adjust their ownership in relation to the expected future performance; Seyhun (1998) provides evidence on this. Himmelberg, Hubbard, and Palia (1999) argue that the ownership structure of the firm may be endogenously determined by the firm's contracting environment, which differs across firms in observable and unobservable ways. For example, if the scope for perquisite consumption is low in a firm, then a low level of management ownership may be the optimal incentive contract.

The endogeneity of management ownership has also been noted by Jensen and Warner (1988, p. 13): "A caveat to the alignment/ entrenchment interpretation of the cross-sectional evidence, however, is that it treats ownership as exogenous, and does not address the issue of what determines ownership concentration for a given firm or why concentration would not be chosen to maximize firm value. Managers and shareholders have incentives to avoid inside ownership stakes in the range where their interests are not aligned, although managerial wealth constraints and benefits from entrenchment could make such holdings efficient for managers."

There is a substantial empirical literature that has studied the relation between corporate ownership and performance. Before reviewing some of this literature, it would be helpful to discuss the empirical proxies for ownership and performance.

2.1.3.2 Empirical Proxies for Corporate Performance   The extant literature has used accounting-based performance measures, such as return on capital, or market-based measures, such as Tobin's q (usually measured as the current market value of the company divided by the replacement cost of the company's asset, which is usually measured as the book value of the company's assets). Market measures of performance could also include the company's stock returns over a period of time (suitably adjusted for size and industry).

If one were interested in the hypothesis that ownership affected performance (in the Granger causality sense) for a sample of companies for a particular year (say, 1995), then one could consider the relationship between ownership and return on capital for some period after 1995 (say, 1996 through 1998). Alternatively, one could consider the average q over from 1996 through 1998 or the company's stock returns from 1996 through 1998. What are the pros and cons of these three measures of performance?

If the stock market is semistrong form efficient, then the stock price in 1995 would anticipate and incorporate the impact of the ownership structure on current and future company performance. One would not observe a significant relationship between ownership and stock returns from 1996 through 1998 *even if ownership had a real impact on performance.*

Tobin's q does not suffer from this anticipation problem but suffers from other equally serious problems. First, the denominator usually does not include the investments a firm may have made in intangible assets. If a firm has a higher fraction of its assets as intangibles, and if monitoring intangible assets is more difficult for the shareholders, then the shareholders are likely to require a higher level of managerial ownership to align the incentives. Since the firm has a higher fraction of its assets as intangibles, it will have a higher q since the numerator (market price) will impound the present value of the cash flows generated by the intangible assets, but the denominator, under current accounting conventions, will not include the replacement value of these intangible assets. These intangible assets will generate a positive correlation between ownership and performance, but this relation is spurious, not causal.

Second, a higher q might be reflective of greater market power. Shareholders, aware that this market power shields the management to a greater degree from the discipline of the product market, will require managers of such a company to own more stock. Greater managerial ownership will tend to align managers' incentives better and offset the effect of the reduced discipline of the product market. In the above scenario, we would again observe a spurious relation between performance as measured by q and managerial ownership. Finally, as suggested by Fershtman and Judd (1987), shareholders may induce the managers (via greater share ownership) to engage in collusive behavior and generate market power. In this scenario, we would also observe a spurious relation between performance as measured by q and managerial ownership.

What about accounting-based measures of performance? Accounting-based performance measures, such as return on assets or return on invested capital, do not suffer from the anticipation problem: accounting performance measures for 1995 will reflect only the performance for 1995. Even if it is known with a high degree of certainty that a company's cash flows will be significantly higher from 1996 through 1998, this fact, by itself, will not lead the accountants to compute a higher accounting performance for 1995. Another advantage of accounting-based performance measures is that they are not affected by market "moods." This argument is, of course, inconsistent with a semistrong, efficient view of the market. Critics of accounting-based performance measures argue that such measures are affected by accounting conventions for valuing assets and revenue; in particular, different methods are applied to value tangible and intangible assets. Also, if management compensation is based on accounting-based performance measures, then managers have an incentive to manipulate these measures. However, while managers can manipulate earnings for a given year, their ability to do so for a longer period, such as five years, is quite limited.

If one were interested in the hypothesis that performance affected ownership (in the Granger causality sense) for a sample of companies for a particular year (say, 1995), then one could consider the relationship between ownership and return on capital for some period prior to 1995 (say, 1991 through 1994). Alternatively, one could consider the average q from 1991 through 1994 or the company's stock returns from 1991 through 1994 as measures of performance.

Kothari and Warner (1997), Barber and Lyon (1997), and Lyon, Barber, and Tsai (1999) have raised serious concerns about the specification and power of the standard methodology to measure "abnormal returns" when long-horizon windows of several years are considered. Kothari and Warner find that the abnormal-return test statistics used in the long-horizon window studies are generally misspecified in the sense that they reject the null hypothesis of normal performance when there is no abnormal performance too frequently given the significance level. Lyon, Barber, and Tsai suggest ways to construct properly specified test statistics. However, these authors caution that while these test statistics appear to be well specified for random samples, they are not well specified for nonrandom samples. Given that tests of most interesting hypotheses are likely to lead to the construction of nonrandom samples, the concern with the misspecification of the long-run test statistics remains. Finally, Lyon, Barber, and Tsai document the power of the long-horizon test statistic to detect abnormal performance when it is actually present. Using state-of-the-art techniques, they find that for a 12-month, buy-and-hold abnormal return, a sample size of 200 firms, and a one-sided test with a 5 percent significance level, the probabilities of detecting an abnormal return of 5 percent, 10 percent, and 20 percent, are 20 percent, 55 percent, and 100 percent, respectively. As the horizon increases beyond 12 months and the sample size decreases, the power of the technique would further diminish. For these reasons, these authors conclude that "the analysis of long-run abnormal returns is treacherous" (Lyon, Barber, and Tsai 1999, p. 198).

What about the specification and power of long-run accounting measures of performance? Barber and Lyon (1996) analyze the specification and power of various accounting-based measures of performance, including return on assets, return on market value of assets, and cash-flow return on assets. For random samples, they find return on sales to be the most powerful for detecting abnormal performance when it actually is present. Their results imply that the abnormal annual return on sales has to increase or decrease by about three cents on each dollar of assets before we can detect it with a high (95 percent) degree of confidence. Given that tests of most interesting hypotheses are likely to lead to the construction of nonrandom samples and that periods greater than a year will be considered, concerns about the power of such long-horizon accounting-based performance measures remain.

2.1.3.3   Extant Literature on Ownership and Performance   An extensive literature considers the relationship between ownership and performance. With rare exceptions, most studies use Tobin's q as the performance measure without considering other accounting- and stock-return-based measures. Our concern (as noted above) regarding the use of Tobin's q as a performance measure, especially when studying its relation to ownership, would apply to most of these studies. Managerial ownership has been measured several different ways—ownership of the board, insider ownership, CEO ownership, and block-holder ownership. The earlier studies did not consider the endogenous relationship between ownership and performance; more recent studies do consider this. While some studies find a nonmonotonic relation between ownership and performance, the evidence viewed in its entirety does not provide strong support for a relation between ownership and performance.

Morck, Shleifer, and Vishny (1988) argue that at low levels of ownership, the incentive effect of ownership would lead to a positive relation between ownership and performance. At higher levels of ownership, managers may feel entrenched in the sense of not being as concerned about losing their jobs subsequent to a proxy fight or takeover; this would lead to a negative relation between ownership and performance. For even greater levels of ownership, the incentive effect of ownership would again dominate and lead to a positive relation between ownership and performance. They measured performance as Tobin's q and ownership as the combined shareholdings of all board members who have a minimum stake of 0.2 percent. They estimate a piecewise linear regression and find a positive relation between ownership and performance for ownership levels between 0 percent and 5 percent, negative between 5 percent and 25 percent, and positive beyond 25 percent. This result is robust to the inclusion of the following control variables: leverage, growth, size, industry dummies, R&D, and advertising ratios. However, their results are not robust to the use of accounting-based performance measures. Also, they do not consider the endogenous nature of the relation between ownership and performance.

McConnell and Servaes (1990) find a positive relation between q and insider ownership for ownership up to 50 percent and then a slight negative relation. These findings are robust to the use of accounting-based measures of performance but not to block ownership as a measure of ownership. They are not able to document the piecewise linear relationship of Morck, Shleifer, and Vishny (1988). Also, they do not consider the endogenous nature of the relationship between ownership and performance.

Hermalin and Weisbach (1991) consider the relationships among ownership, board structure, and performance. They consider the ownership of the present CEO and any previous CEO still on the board. Board structure is measured as the fraction of board consisting of outsiders, and performance is measured as Tobin's q. They consider ownership and board structure as endogenous by using their lagged values as instruments. They find a nonmonotonic relation between ownership and performance: positive between 0 percent and 1 percent, negative between 1 percent and 5 percent, positive between 5 percent and 20 percent, and negative beyond 20 percent.

Loderer and Martin (1997) construct a simultaneous-equations model where they treat performance and ownership as endogenous for a sample of acquisitions. Performance is measured as q, and ownership is measured as the percentage ownership of all officers and directors. Insider ownership is not a significant predictor of q, but q is a significant negative predictor of insider ownership.

Cho (1998) constructs a three-equation simultaneous-equations model where performance, ownership, and corporate investment are treated as endogenous. Performance is measured as q, ownership is measured as the percentage ownership of all officers and directors, and investments are measured as capital expenditures (alternatively, as R&D) as a fraction of total assets. Performance is a positive predictor of ownership. Ownership does not predict performance, but investment is a positive predictor.

Himmelberg, Hubbard, and Palia (1999) use a fixed-effects panel data model and instrumental variables to control for unobserved firm heterogeneity. Tobin's q is the proxy for performance, and insider equity ownership is the ownership proxy. They find that ownership has a quadratic relationship with firm size and has a negative relation with the ratio of tangible assets to sales and the firm's idiosyncratic risk. Controlling for these variables and firm fixed effects, they do not find a relationship between ownership and performance. However, when they control for endogeneity of ownership using instrumental variables, they observe a quadratic relationship between ownership and performance.

Demsetz and Villalonga (2001) emphasize the endogeneity of the ownership structure. They measure performance as q and an accounting-based performance measure. Ownership is measured two different ways: average ownership of the CEO and all board members owning more than 0.02 percent and the fraction of shares owned by the five largest shareholders. They estimate a two-equations model using two-stage least squares and find that ownership is negatively related to debt ratio, unsystematic risk, and performance. However, performance is not influenced by ownership.

2.1.4 Relational Investors and Corporate Performance

American public corporations have long been characterized by a relative absence of influential shareholders who hold large blocks of a company's stock for a long period of time and actively monitor its performance (sometimes called *relational investors*). The resulting separation of ownership and control has formed the dominant paradigm for understanding our corporate governance system for most of this century (Berle and Means 1932; see Jensen and Meckling 1976). But the weak shareholder oversight that is the U.S. norm is not inevitable. Internationally, the United States is unique in the weakness of even the largest shareholders in its major firms. The absence of such investors in the United States, despite the presence of strong bank shareholders in Germany and Japan, is perhaps the single defining difference between the capital markets of these three major economies. Moreover, the weakness of American shareholders may reflect the political decisions that kept them small and passive rather than the survival of efficient shareholding patterns in a competitive marketplace (Black 1990; Roe 1994).

The combination of American exceptionalism in having weak shareholders and the possible political origins of that exceptionalism raises important policy questions: Would there be economic benefits from relaxing the legal rules that discourage institutional investors from holding large blocks and intervening actively when management falters? Or has the United States evolved substitute oversight mechanisms that accomplish much the same job that relational investors accomplish elsewhere? If so, adding relational investing to our current corporate governance system wouldn't significantly affect firm performance. If institutions were invited to become relational investors by more favorable legal rules, would they accept the invitation?

One potential advantage of a governance system in which more firms have relational investors derives from concerns that managers and shareholders may focus excessively on short-term profitability, with a resulting cost in long-term performance (for example, Jacobs 1991; Porter 1992). This myopic manager/shareholder argument is inconsistent with the semistrong form of the efficient market hypothesis: markets would impound the impact of corporate decisions on the share price *today* from future cash flows—whether these cash flows occur next year, three years from now, or 30 years from now. The theoretical basis for the myopic manager/shareholder concern can be stated as such: if investors have imperfect information about a company's prospects, they may rely on short-term earnings as the best available signal of those prospects. Managers may also overemphasize short-term results, either to please myopic shareholders or simply to earn this year's bonus (for example, Shleifer and Vishny 1990; Stein 1989, 1996). Alternatively, managers may invest in poor long-term projects if they believe that shareholders will reward this behavior with higher short-term stock prices (Bebchuk and Stole 1993). Large shareholders can invest in monitoring, thus reducing the information asymmetry that drives shareholder and manager myopia in these models.

Relational investing could also serve as a substitute for, or complement to, the market for corporate control. In the 1980s, hostile takeovers were an important source of monitoring and disciplining corporate managers (for example, Jensen 1986; Mikkelson and Partch 1997). However, hostile takeovers are highly costly and are feasible only if there is a large gap between a company's value under current management and its potential value if sold or better managed. Moreover, hostile takeovers are now less prevalent, partly because they are chilled by legal rules that give managers great discretion to block unwanted takeovers (however, see Comment and Schwert 1995). Relational investors potentially could both provide monitoring in normal times (when a firm is not performing badly enough to warrant a hostile takeover bid) and act as a counterweight to management's incentives to block value-enhancing control changes.

At the same time, strong outside shareholders are not an unmitigated blessing. Because they own large stakes, they can overcome the collective-action problems that make small shareholders passive and the information asymmetry that may make small shareholders myopic. But large shareholders can also take advantage of their influence and the passivity of other shareholders to extract private benefits from the corporation. For example, a bank that is both a major shareholder and a lender to a company may discourage risk taking to protect its position as creditor or may cause the company to borrow from the bank when cheaper financing is available elsewhere. Moreover, institutional investors are themselves managed by agents who face their own agency costs and may not maximize the value of the institution's stake in a portfolio company (Black 1992a; Black and Coffee 1994; Fisch 1994; Romano 1993). In light of the risks posed by overly strong shareholders, Black (1992a) has previously argued that ownership of moderately large blocks (in the 5 to 10 percent range) by a half dozen institutions might produce better governance outcomes than ownership of very large blocks (say, 20 percent or more) by one or two major shareholders. Hence, any correlation between relational investing and performance could be nonmonotonic: relational investing might produce benefits up to one ownership level and costs above that level.

Finally, relational investing is only one of a myraid of mechanisms that have evolved to align the interests of managers with that of shareholders. Others include management compensation contracts that emphasize equity-sensitive claims, the corporate control market (takeovers, proxy fights), various corporate governance mechanisms such as oversight and monitoring by board members, and finally the discipline of competition in the product market. Thus, from a theoretical perspective, relational investing could be a complement to these monitoring mechanisms and would serve to improve performance. Or the above monitoring mechanisms, either individually or in combination, could be a perfect substitute for relational investing; in this case relational investing would not affect performance. Thus, whether relational investing will improve or degrade corporate performance or will not affect performance strongly one way or another is uncertain as a theoretical matter; the empirical literature is also inconclusive.

A variety of evidence, some systematic and some anecdotal, has been cited in support of the view that relational investing could improve corporate performance. Some advocates of relational investing draw inferences from descriptions by business historians of the roles that large investors have played in particular companies, such as Pierre DuPont at General Motors, J. P. Morgan and his associates in companies in which they had invested, and, in contemporary times, Warren Buffett at Salomon Brothers (see, for example, Lowenstein 1991). Kleiman, Nathan, and Shulman (1994) report more generally, but still anecdotally, that negotiated large-block investments, some by self-styled "relationship investing" funds, generally predict positive market-adjusted stock price returns but *not* when the target obtains the investment as part of a defense to a takeover bid.

Direct, quantitative evidence about the impact that large investors have on corporate behavior and performance can be divided into four types: evidence on the impact of majority shareholdings, evidence on the impact of large block holdings by corporate insiders, evidence on the impact of large minority-block shareholding by outsiders, and, finally, evidence on the impact of institutional investors. While the third and fourth types are most relevant to the debate over relational investing, most research has focused on the first two categories. We summarize the literature here:

• *On majority or control-block holdings* An early study by McEachern (1975) finds weak evidence that firms with a controlling shareholder are more profitable than manager-controlled firms. Salancik and Pfeffer (1980) find that CEO tenure correlates with firm profitability for firms with a controlling shareholder but not for other firms. Holderness and Sheehan (1985) find that an outsider's purchase of a majority block, without announced plans for a complete takeover, produces a 9.4 percent stock price gain over a 30-day window. However, they find no significant differences in Tobin's q or accounting measures of profitability between majority-owned and diffusely owned firms.

• *On large block holdings by corporate insiders* The correlation between inside ownership and profitability remains controversial in the literature, and the results are sensitive to whether management ownership is treated as exogenous or endogenous (as already discussed in detail above). Companies with high inside ownership are more likely than manager-controlled companies to agree to a friendly acquisition and are less likely to expand sales at the expense of profits. Also, bidders with high inside ownership make fewer conglomerate acquisitions, make better acquisitions generally, and pay lower takeover premiums (see the survey by Black 1992b).

• *On large minority-block holdings by outsiders* Mikkelson and Ruback (1985) and others find increases in the value of target firms on the announcement that an investor has taken a large-block position, but most of the positive returns are explained by anticipation of a subsequent takeover of the firm. The gains are reversed for firms that are not subsequently acquired. However, Barclay and Holderness (1992) find a market-adjusted increase in the price of the remaining publicly traded shares after a transaction in which a large block of shares is acquired at a premium, both for firms that are acquired within one year and for firms that are not acquired, though the increase is smaller for the nonacquired group.

  Gordon and Pound (1992) study a small sample (18) of "patient capital investments," which they define as transactions in which an investment partnership purchases a new block of equity and is granted at least one seat on the board. Together, Warren Buffett and Corporate Partners Fund account for about half of their sample. They find that "patient capital" investing has not produced returns that are statistically different from the S&P 500.

Bhagat and Jefferis (1994) investigate targeted share repurchases or "greenmail" transactions where managers agree to repurchase a block of shares at a premium from a single shareholder or group of shareholders. They find that performance of firms that pay greenmail cannot be distinguished from a control group—before or after the repurchase.

Fleming (1993) finds that investors who acquired a large equity stake between 1985 and 1989 in a firm that was not subsequently acquired did little to affect the firm's performance. He finds significant positive returns for the target company's shares during the first two months after the the investor's purchase but significant negative returns over the subsequent two years. Much of Fleming's sample consists of large-block acquisitions by corporate "raiders" and arbitrageurs such as Victor Posner and Ivan Boesky.

Bethel, Liebeskind, and Opler (1998) examine purchases of large blocks of stock by activist investors during the 1980s. These purchases were followed by abnormal share-price appreciation, an increase in asset divestitures, an increase in operating profitability, and a decrease in merger and acquisition activity.

• *On the impact of institutional investors*   Wahal and McConnell (1999) report that firms with high institutional ownership invest more heavily in R&D, consistent with reduced information asymmetry leading to reduced managerial myopia. Also, higher institutional ownership correlates with lower bid-ask spreads for Nasdaq stocks from 1983 through 1991 and that a smaller proportion of this spread is attributable to informational asymmetry. Denis, Denis, and Sarin (1997) report that the presence of an outside block holder correlates with higher top-executive turnover, and with a stronger correlation between turnover and poor firm performance. However, none of these studies explores the impact of institutional ownership on overall firm performance.

A number of studies examine the impact of institutional activism on the performance of the targeted firm and collectively find only limited evidence that activism improves subsequent performance or affects the firm's subsequent actions (see the survey in Black 1998).

In sum, the extant evidence provides modest evidence that large-block investments by insiders (management) or by outsiders can increase firm value. There is considerable variance in this finding, however. Most studies discussed above are based on relatively small

samples over relatively short time periods—perhaps too short for
the hypothesized effects of relational investing to show up. Many
examine investment by a corporate "raider"—the antithesis of the
model that proponents of relational investing have in mind.

Finally, with the exception of Carleton, Nelson, and Weisbach
(1998), previous researchers have looked for evidence of performance effects from certain actions that investors or investor groups
take (for example, the filing of shareholder resolutions, the targeting
of a firm for takeover by activist investors, or the targeting of poor
performers with negative publicity campaigns by groups such as the
Council of Institutional Investors). While these studies are helpful in
understanding the market's valuation of certain block-holder actions,
they may entirely miss the essence of the way relationship investing
is supposed to work. Specifically, relational investors are supposed
to work constructively with management—not under media glare or
with much, if any, public disclosure. Given the above consideration,
the only way to determine the impact of relational investors on firm
performance is to consider performance over long horizons of several years.

Bhagat, Black, and Blair (2001) propose operational definitions of
the concept of relational investing and have conducted the first large-
scale test of the hypothesis that relational investing can improve the
performance of U.S. firms. They collect ownership and performance
data on more than 1,500 of the largest U.S. companies over a 13-year
period (1983 through 1995). They describe the patterns of long-term,
large-block shareholding among large, publicly traded companies.
They document a significant secular increase in large-block shareholding over the period of study, with sharp percentage increases in
holdings by mutual funds, partnerships, investment advisors, and
employee benefit plans. However, most institutional investors, when
they purchase large blocks, sell the blocks relatively quickly—too
quickly to be considered relational investors.

Their results provide a mixed answer to the question of whether
relational investing affects corporate performance. Their data suggest that the cohort of relational investors (defined generally as outside shareholders who hold a 10 percent stake for at least four years)
who held their positions from 1987 through 1990 often targeted firms
that had been growing rapidly during the previous four-year period.
During the 1987 through 1990 period, firms with relational investors
outperformed their peers using stock-price returns and Tobin's q as

performance measures. This is consistent with these investors' having helped their target companies to translate strong growth in the prior (1983 through 1986) period into strong earnings and rising stock prices. But this pattern was not found in the early 1980s or repeated in the early 1990s.

Thus, their data suggest that there may have been a cohort of relational investors who identified a successful investment strategy or were able to encourage restructuring that improved the performance of their target companies. That strategy could have depended on an active market for hostile takeovers and leveraged restructurings—a market that flourished during the 1987 through 1990 period, was less active in the 1983 through 1986 period, and all but disappeared in the first half of the 1990s. Their data do not suggest that relational investing gives firms a sustainable competitive advantage in an environment of few hostile takeovers and equity prices such that leveraged restructurings are unattractive.

Also, Bhagat, Black, and Blair (2001) emphasize that the idea of relational investing must be more carefully specified and clarified in theory. Although their findings are discouraging for a simple-minded theory that large-block shareholders are better monitors and therefore induce better performance, they leave open the possibility that some kinds of investors might have more effect than others. Ownership of a large block of shares by an officer or director might have a different effect than ownership of a similarly large block by a pension fund or mutual fund. And ownership by an employee stock ownership plan might have yet a different effect. Quiet, steady ownership may have a different impact on performance than noisy, activist ownership.

2.1.5   *Corporate Governance and Ownership Structure*

The corporate charter is a contract that governs relations between managers and shareholders. Most earlier studies of management-sponsored antitakeover amendments adopted by the shareholders focused mainly on the wealth effects associated with the amendments and secondarily on the ownership structure of the firms that adopted them. The accumulated evidence on the impact of these amendments on shareholder wealth is weak, with point estimates that range from slightly negative to slightly positive (see DeAngelo and Rice 1983 and Linn and McConnell 1983). Using a 31-day window, Jarrell and

Poulsen (1987) identify wealth effects that are negative and statistically significant for some types of amendments and effects that are negative but not statistically significant in shorter return windows. In assessing the Jarrell and Poulsen 31-day returns, it would be useful to reconsider the power and specification concerns about the long-window abnormal returns statistic as highlighted by Barber and Lyon (1997) and Kothari and Warner (1997) above.

Ownership data in firms that propose such amendments and voting patterns on these amendments suggest that the amendments are supported by corporate insiders and opposed by the typical institutional investor. Brickley, Lease, and Smith (1988) document voting patterns consistent with the hypothesis that institutional investors are more likely than non-block-holding investors to oppose antitakeover amendments, while corporate insiders support the adoption of amendments. Jarrell and Poulsen (1987) report above-average insider holdings and below-average institutional holdings in a large sample of firms that enact amendments. A plausible interpretation is that antitakeover amendments protect managers from the discipline of the takeover market while harming shareholders.

There are, however, reasonable arguments to support the view that management-sponsored antitakeover amendments do not actually injure shareholders. The notion that antitakeover amendments increase managers' bargaining power is inconsistent with Pound's (1987) finding that antitakeover amendments do not increase bid premiums. A second argument—that managers of firms adopting amendments are simply enjoying contractual protection against takeovers afforded them by shareholders—is consistent with the fact that shareholders vote to approve the overwhelming majority of proposals put forth by management. Jarrell, Brickley, and Netter (1988) attribute shareholder support for wealth-decreasing amendments to the free-rider problem. Bhagat and Jefferis (1991) argue that the transaction costs that give rise to the free-rider problem are, at least in part, an endogenous consequence of strategic behavior that might be eliminated through either changes in the charter or proxy reform.

Bhagat and Jefferis (1991) construct an econometric methodology that incorporates both prior information about the likelihood of adoption and the returns realized by firms that might have enacted amendments but did not do so. They estimate a wealth effect on the order of negative 1 percent of equity value for a large sample of firms that adopted antitakeover amendments in 1984 and 1985. The effect is statistically significant and consistent across different types of amendments, including fair-price amendments. They document a relationship between the distribution of announcement returns and the prior probability of announcement; this suggests that anticipation attenuates announcement effects. They also find that returns of nonproposing firms contain information about the effects of antitakeover amendments; this suggests a sample-selection bias in most studies that have investigated the wealth effects of antitakeover charter amendments.

Bhagat and Jefferis (1991) address the self-selection bias issue by considering the difference in ownership structure between firms that enact amendments and those that do not. They find that aversion of certain firms to antitakeover amendments persists outside the sample period, suggesting genuine differences between the two samples. They find that the fraction of total votes controlled by the CEO is negatively related to the likelihood that an amendment will be proposed, as is the fraction of votes controlled by officers and directors and the voting power of outside directors. The marginal effect on the likelihood of enactment of block ownership by corporate officers is negative when the effect of other ownership characteristics is constrained to zero but positive when this constraint is relaxed. This suggests that officers who are block holders tend to oppose amendments but are less vigorous in their opposition than officers who are not block holders. Most officers who are also block holders are members of the firms' founding families. In many cases, proxy documents reveal that a relative of the block holder is also an officer of the corporation. This block holder profile is consistent with the evidence presented by Morck, Shleifer, and Vishny (1989), who note that the presence of a member of the founding family on the top management team has a negative impact on the likelihood of both a hostile takeover and top management turnover.

2.1.6 Takeovers, Management Turnover, Performance, and Ownership

Martin and McConnell (1991) study performance prior to and managerial turnover subsequent to 253 successful tender-offer takeovers for a sample of NYSE firms from 1958 through 1984. They measure performance using market-adjusted and industry-adjusted stock returns for the 48-month period prior to the tender offer. They classify their takeover as disciplinary if there is turnover of the top manager of the target firm within a year of the takeover. They find that takeover targets are from industries that are performing well relative to the market and that targets of disciplinary takeovers are performing poorly within their industry. During the year subsequent to the takeover, they document a rate of management turnover of 42 percent compared to an annual rate of about 10 percent in the five-year period prior to the tender offer.

DeAngelo and DeAngelo (1989) study management turnover subsequent to 60 proxy contests in NYSE and AMEX firms from 1978 through 1985. The cumulative survival rate for incumbent management in these 60 firms one year after the proxy contest outcome (regardless of the outcome) is 28 percent, and three years after the contest the outcome is 18 percent.

Ikenberry and Lakonishok (1993) study the performance of 97 firms subject to proxy contests before and subsequent to the contest from 1968 through 1987. Both stock-market- and accounting-based performance measures indicate poor performance five years prior to the proxy contest. Also, accounting-based performance measures indicate poor performance five years subsequent to the proxy contest, especially if dissidents win.

Bhagat and Jefferis (1994) study the frequency of executive turnover in a sample of 110 firms that paid greenmail from 1974 through 1983. Greenmail or targeted repurchase refers to the purchase of a block of shares by the company at a premium from a single shareholder or group of shareholders; this offer is not made to all shareholders. The motivation for paying greenmail is alleged to be deterrence of a takeover on terms that would be unfavorable to incumbent management. They find management turnover is less frequent at repurchasing firms than control firms of similar size and industry. This is true unconditionally and for a subsample of firms that do not experience a takeover. However, they argue that takeovers and managerial turnover are endogenous. Less frequent management turnover at repurchasing firms may suggest that managers of those firms are insulated from market discipline. Alternatively, it may be the case that managerial performance at repurchasing firms does not warrant discipline: they find that accounting-based performance measures for firms that paid greenmail and the control sample are similar both prior to and subsequent to the repurchase.

Denis and Serrano (1996) study management turnover following 98 unsuccessful control contests from 1983 through 1989. Thirty-four percent of these firms experience management turnover from the initiation of the control contest through two years following resolution of the contest. This rate of management turnover is twice that of a random sample of firms during the same period. Further, they find that turnover is concentrated in poorly performing firms in which investors unaffiliated with management purchase large blocks of shares during and subsequent to the control contest. In contrast, managers of firms with no unaffiliated block purchases appear to be able to extend their tenure despite an equally poor performance prior to the control contest. They also find improved performance in firms experiencing turnover and continued poor performance in firms where managers were able to stay in power.

Denis, Denis, and Sarin (1997) study the impact of ownership structure on management turnover in a sample of 1,394 firms from 1985 through 1988. They find that management turnover is more likely as the equity ownership of officers and directors decreases and whether or not there is an outside block holder. They also document evidence suggesting that the impact of managerial ownership on turnover may be due, in part, to the impact of managerial ownership on corporate control activity; they observe a significantly higher occurrence of corporate control activity in the year prior to the management turnover, regardless of the level of management ownership.

Mikkelson and Partch (1997) study the impact of performance on management turnover during an active takeover market in the United States (1984 through 1988) compared to a less active takeover market (1989 through 1993) for a sample of unacquired firms. They find the frequency of managerial turnover is significantly higher during the active takeover market compared to the less active takeover market. Additionally, this decline in the frequency of managerial turnover is most conspicuous among poorly performing firms.

2.1.7 Capital Structure, Managerial Incentives, and Ownership Structure

In a seminal paper, Grossman and Hart (1983) considered the ex ante efficiency perspective to derive predictions about a firm's financing decisions in an agency setting. An initial entrepreneur seeks to maximize firm value with some disciplinary mechanism that forces the entrepreneur to choose the value-maximizing level of debt. Novaes and Zingales (1999) show that the optimal choice of debt from the viewpoint of shareholders differs from the optimal choice of debt from the viewpoint of managers. The conflict of interest between managers and shareholders over financing policy arises for three reasons: shareholders are much better diversified than managers, who besides having stock and stock options on the firm have their human capital tied to the firm (Fama, 1980); as suggested by Jensen (1986), a larger level of debt precommits the manager to working harder to generate and pay off the firm's cash flows to outside investors; and Harris and Raviv (1988) and Stulz (1988) argue that managers may increase leverage beyond what might be implied by some "optimal capital structure" to increase the voting power of their equity stakes and reduce the likelihood of a takeover and the resulting possible loss of job tenure.

Berger, Ofek, and Yermack (1997) document that managerial entrenchment has a significant impact on firms' capital structures. They find lower leverage in firms where the CEO appears to be entrenched: in these situations, CEOs have had a long tenure in office, and their compensation plans are not closely linked to firm performance. Also, they find lower leverage in firms where the CEO does not face significant monitoring: in these situations, boards are large and have few outside directors, and there are no large outside block holders. Most notably, they document that firms that experience some discipline (such as a takeover attempt, an involuntary CEO departure, or the arrival of an outside block holder) or improved managerial incentives through the management compensation contract significantly increase their leverage.

While the above focuses on capital structure and managerial entrenchment, a different strand of the literature has focused on the relation between capital structure and ownership structure. Grossman and Hart (1986) and Hart and Moore (1990) consider an incomplete contracting environment—where it is difficult to specify all possible future states of nature and relevant decisions in a contract that can be enforced in a court. In such an incomplete contracting environment, ex ante allocation of control rights could be used to provide incentives to managers to make firm-specific human capital investments. While there is an extensive literature on capital structure and security design (see Harris and Raviv 1991, 1992), Mahrt-Smith (2000) provides the most relevant analysis of the relation between capital structure and ownership structure.

Mahrt-Smith (2000) considers stockholders and bondholders that have differential ability to monitor managers and managers who have a preference for which of these two types of investors should have the legal control rights to the firm. In this scenario, a contract could be designed that leaves the manager's preferred investor group in charge when the manager's performance is better than some verifiable benchmark. What determines the ability of shareholders and bondholders to differentially monitor managers? Monitoring ability is determined by a concentration of ownership, monitoring incentives and abilities of investors, board representation, corporate charter provisions, bond covenants, and the propensity of courts to differentially weigh shareholder and bondholder rights. Managers will prefer dispersed stockholders over concentrated and strong bondholders—especially if these bondholders have covenants and courts on their side and they sit on the board. As stockownership gets too dispersed, managers may use their greater discretionary authority to engage in self-serving behavior, and this would lead to a drop in the value of the claims on the firm that would ultimately be borne by themselves (managers)—as pointed out by Jensen and Meckling (1976). Thus managers will experience a tradeoff between very strong bondholders and very weak shareholders.

2.2   Cross-Sectional Models and Identification

In the corporate governance environment discussed above, an econometric model for investigating, say, the impact of takeover defense on takeover activity has the following structure:

$$Separation = f_1(Governance, Ownership, Performance, Z_1, \varepsilon_1) \qquad (2.1)$$

$$Governance = f_2(Ownership, Performance, Z_2, \varepsilon_2) \qquad (2.2)$$

$$Ownership = f_3(Governance, Performance, Z_3, \varepsilon_3) \qquad (2.3)$$

$$Performance = f_4(Governance, Ownership, Z_4, \varepsilon_4). \qquad (2.4)$$

In equations (2.1) through (2.4), *Separation* is a mnemonic for *takeovers or managerial turnover; Governance* refers to *takeover defense, corporate board structure,* and *board and management compensation structures; Ownership* refers to *equity ownership and capital structure of the firm;* the Z_i are vectors of instruments that affect the dependent variable; and the error terms ε_i are associated with exogenous noise and the unobservable features of managerial behavior or ability that explain cross-sectional variation in ownership and takeover defense. The moments of the performance distribution are reflected in contract provisions like ownership and takeover defense. *The incentive-based explanation of takeover activity, managerial turnover, and takeover defense implies that all of these variables are determined simultaneously.*

The above system of equations, when identified and estimated, can answer many interesting questions in corporate governance:

· What is the impact of takeover defenses on managerial tenure?

· What is the impact of capital structure on the likelihood of a takeover attempt and on managerial tenure?

· What is the impact of management ownership on firm performance?

· What is the impact of corporate performance on the likelihood of a takeover attempt? What is the impact of block-holder ownership on the likelihood of a takeover attempt being successful?

· What is the impact of corporate performance on the structure of the corporate board?

· What is the impact of corporate performance on management, board, and block-holder ownership?

· What is the impact of board structure on corporate performance?

· What is the impact of capital structure on corporate performance?

Equation (2.1) considers the impact of takeover defenses on the likelihood of a takeover and managerial tenure. Pound's (1987) study of the effect of takeover defense is a univariate version of this model, where ownership, performance, and Z_1 are suppressed. The omission of these variables biases the estimate of the impact of takeover defense on the frequency of takeover activity when the presence of takeover defenses is correlated with ownership and performance. Takeover defenses affect turnover through the impact of performance on takeover defenses (equation (2.2)); managers of poorly performing firms are more likely to erect takeover defenses. Such defenses might discourage an outsider from accumulating a block of shares in this company, with a corresponding decrease in the probability of dismissal of poorly performing managers. Denis, Denis, and Sarin (1997), Allen (1981), and Salancik and Pfeffer (1980) document correlations between ownership and management turnover.

Econometric models that acknowledge the possibility that performance and ownership influence separations do not necessarily yield consistent estimates for the parameters of interest. Identification requires some combination of exclusion restrictions, assumptions about the joint distribution of the error terms, and restrictions on the functional form of the f_i. Maddala (1983) discusses restrictions that identify the model when the ε_i are normally distributed. Identification in *single-equation* semiparametric index models—where the functional form of f_1 is unknown and the explanatory variables in that equation are continuous, known functions of a basic parameter vector—is discussed by Ichimura and Lee (1991). Estimation of a system of the form of equations (2.1) through (2.4) in the absence of strong restrictions on *both* the f_i and the joint distribution of error terms is, to the best of our knowledge, an unsolved problem.

We are unaware of a model of takeover defense that implies specific functional forms for the f_i. If these functions are linear, identification may be attained through either strong distributional assumptions or exclusion restrictions. Maddala (1983) and Amemiya (1985) discuss restrictions on the ε_i that identify the model in the absence of exclusion restrictions. But these restrictions are inconsistent with incentive-based explanations of takeover defense, since unobservable characteristics of managerial behavior or type will be reflected in all of the ε_i. Using panel data and firm-fixed effects, it would be possible to control for unobservable characteristics of managerial behavior or type; however, a system such as in (2.1) through (2.4) would have to be specified and estimated. Aside from the nontrivial data collection effort required to estimate such a system, this system would not be identified when $Z_2 = Z_3 = Z_4$. Exclusion restrictions are therefore the most likely path to identification.

The hypothesis that we wish to test—do takeover defenses affect the likelihood of takeover activity and managerial turnover?—suggests that exclusion restrictions would be difficult to justify. Intuitively, variables that affect the likelihood of a takeover will be reflected in the structure of takeover defenses. A detailed microeconomic model, based on specific assumptions about preferences and production possibilities, might yield exclusion restrictions. But we are unaware of any candidates and suspect that the same features of the data that yield identification (for example, a Cobb-Douglas production technology) would render the model inconsistent with the data (see Griliches and Mairesse 1999). In the absence of distributional assumptions or functional form restrictions, the econometric model (2.1) through (2.4) is not identified when $Z_2 = Z_3 = Z_4$.

If we ignore these issues and simply write down an econometric model that is identified, estimation is still problematical. Evaluation of the likelihood function requires either the calculation of a two-dimensional numerical integral or simulated moments estimation. The available evidence indicates that either method would require more than 344 observations (our sample size; see chapter 3 for details) to yield meaningful estimates (see McFadden 1989, and Pakes and Pollard 1989). In our initial approach to this problem, we estimated different specifications of the system (2.1) through (2.4) based on exclusion restrictions and distributional assumptions. We found the results of this exercise to be uninformative. The likelihood function is flat, suggesting that the model is poorly specified.

2.3 Dummy Variable Regressions

An econometric model of the form (2.1) through (2.4) reveals the effect of performance and ownership on separations when the model is identified. In the absence of identification, we cannot give a causal interpretation to parameter estimates. When the model is not identified, statements like the following are not internally consistent: "At firms with no takeover defenses, a 5 percent deviation in performance three years in a row is associated with an increased frequency of managerial turnover. The same deviation in performance is not associated with managerial turnover at firms that have takeover defenses. Therefore, removing takeover defenses would strengthen the link between performance and managerial turnover." The inference in the third sentence is not warranted by the observations in the first two sentences unless the model is identified.

It is, however, possible to contrast the experience and characteristics of firms that have takeover defenses with the experience and characteristics of firms that do not have takeover defenses. We analyze the relationship between takeover defense, separations, and performance with some dummy variable regressions that speak to the significance of omitting ownership and performance from equation (2.1). In these models, ownership and performance are regressed on interactive dummies that describe the experience of sample firms with respect to separations and takeover defense. The estimated coefficients represent the difference in performance (and ownership) between firms that experience separations and firms that do not experience separations, as a function of takeover defense.

A stylized version of the regression model is

$$Performance = \beta_0 + x_1\beta_1 + x_2\beta_2 + \varepsilon, \qquad (2.5)$$

where

$$x_1 = \begin{cases} 1 & \text{if a firm experiences no management} \\ & \text{turnover and has takeover defenses,} \\ 0 & \text{otherwise} \end{cases} \qquad (2.6)$$

$$x_2 = \begin{cases} 1 & \text{if a firm experiences no management} \\ & \text{turnover and has no takeover defenses,} \\ 0 & \text{otherwise.} \end{cases} \qquad (2.7)$$

The estimated value of β_1 (and β_2) represents the mean deviation in performance between type 1 (and type 2) firms as noted in (2.6) (and (2.7)) and all firms that experience management turnover. Positive estimates are consistent with performance-based explanations of turnover. The difference between β_1 and β_2 illustrates the contrast in performance between firms that have takeover defenses and firms that do not have takeover defenses, conditioned on no management turnover. Explanations of takeover defense based on "management entrenchment" suggest that $\beta_1 > \beta_2$, although the identification issue clouds this interpretation.

We estimate the model using different measures of performance and ownership as the dependent variable. The set of explanatory variables is expanded to accommodate different types of takeover defense, specified so that the x_i are a mutually exclusive and collectively exhaustive partition of either the firms that experience no management turnover or the firms that experience no takeover activity. We specify the explanatory variables in this manner to preserve degrees of freedom: if the dummies represent firms that experience a particular type of takeover activity, such as nonhostile takeovers, instead of firms that experience no takeovers, there are not sufficient observations in individual cells to permit estimation.

2.4 Probit Models and Score Estimators

The specification of equation 2.1 that we estimate is designed to highlight the influence of takeover defense on the relationship between (1) performance and separations and (2) ownership and separations. We choose as explanatory variables a set of interactive terms of the form *dummy_i ∗ performance* and *dummy_i ∗ ownership*. In these expressions, $dummy_i$ is a dummy variable for the ith type of takeover defense. The set of dummies is a mutually exclusive and collectively exhaustive partition of the set of takeover defenses. (If we considered only a single type of defense, there would be two dummies associated with the performance variable—one for firms with that takeover defense and one for firms without that takeover defense.) The hypothesis that the relationship between performance and separations is independent of takeover defense implies that the regression coefficients associated with the interactive variables based on performance should be independent of $dummy_i$. We present a number of different test statistics that address this hypothesis.

Equation 2.1 may be estimated directly under the maintained assumption that defense, performance, and ownership are exogenous. If we assume that f_1 is linear and the latent error term ε_1 is normally distributed, the model is a probit. The probit estimator is the value of β that maximizes the likelihood function

$$\Phi(x\beta)^{s_i}[1 - \Phi(x\beta)]^{1-s_i}, \tag{2.8}$$

where $\Phi(\cdot)$ is the normal cumulative density function (C.D.F.) and the s_i has a value of 1 if a separation occurs and a value of 0 if no separation occurs for firm i. These estimates are biased and inconsistent if the latent error terms are heteroscedastic; the bias may be severe. In a probit model, the data are assumed to be generated by a latent variable y^* such that $y^* = x\beta - u$. The probability that $y^* > 0$ is equal to the probability that $u < x\beta$. This implies that $Pr(y = 1) = \Phi(x\beta)$. If the data-generating process is heteroscedastic, error terms have the form $h(x)u$ and the probability model is $Pr(y = 1) = \Phi((x\beta)/(h(x)))$. If we ignore the heteroscedasticity and calculate $\Phi(x_i\beta)$, the estimator is inconsistent.

Manski and Thompson (1986) analyze the bias empirically for the case where $\Phi(\cdot)$ is logistic rather than normal.

Manski's (1975) score estimator provides consistent estimates of β^*, a normalized version of β that has unit length, under very weak assumptions about the distribution of the ε_i. The score estimator is the value of β that maximizes the criterion function

$$\sum_{j=1}^{n} y_j^* \, sgn(x_j\beta). \tag{2.9}$$

The score estimator does not produce an intercept term. Slope coefficients are identified only up to a scale factor. As a result, evidence from the score model is informative only about the relative magnitude of different parameters. The score model serves mainly as a diagnostic for the probit estimates.

We maximize the criterion function 2.9. There is, to the best of our knowledge, no distribution theory available for the score estimator. Test statistics are calculated with the bootstrap, as in Manski and Thompson (1986).

2.5   The Bootstrap and Weighting to Correct for Stratified Sampling

Our parameter estimates and test statistics are calculated with the bootstrap, as described by Efron (1979). We estimate each model 200 times using a different permutation of the sample on each trial. The collection of parameter estimates from the different trials comprises the sampling distribution of the estimator. For the regression models, the main impact of bootstrap estimation is to reduce the influence of outliers. The contribution of the bootstrap is more substantial in the case of the probit model, where the standard estimator for the parameter covariance matrix is based on asymptotic distribution theory. Test statistics calculated with the bootstrap are linked to the data and are independent of the rate at which the estimator of the parameter covariance matrix converges to its limiting value.

We designed our sample to maximize the range of takeover defenses among sample firms. This enhances the efficiency of estimators for cross-sectional parameters but also biases parameter estimates. A correction for the bias induced by stratified sampling is described by Manski and Lerman (1977). The efficiency gains from stratified sampling and the bias correction are discussed in Amemiya (1985).

We consider two types of weighting schemes. In the qualitative-response models, weights are determined by the frequency of the event that defines the dependent variable. Let w denote the fraction of firms that experience the event in the choice-based sample and z denote the fraction of firms that experience the event in a random sample. To correct the bias induced by the sampling rule, the likelihood function for each observation from the choice-based sample is weighted by w/z, and the likelihood function for each observation from the random sample is weighted by $(1-w)/(1-z)$. The second group of firms in our choice-based sample is not in fact random, since we obtained this group by sampling without replacement from the CRSP tape. A sensitivity analysis reveals that our conclusions are insensitive to the values of these weights.

In the regression models, a response-based analysis is not available. A Bayesian approach to the data would enable us to correct the bias introduced by stratified sampling. As an alternative, we estimate regression models where observations are assigned weights depending on whether the observation is drawn from the random sample or the biased sample. A sensitivity analysis reveals that our conclusions are insensitive to the values of these weights.

3 Sample Construction and Data

The design of the sample is best understood if we first describe its use. We pick a proxy mailing date (which is not the same date in calendar time for all sample firms) and identify the status of takeover defenses at sample firms as of the mailing date. We then identify corporate takeover defenses in place as of the mailing date, ownership structure as of the mailing date, and performance during various periods prior to the mailing date. These are the factors that we believe, on the basis of the extant literature, may influence managerial turnover and takeover activity. We then examine takeover activity and managerial turnover during a two-year period subsequent to the mailing date and correlate the experience of firms and their managers with takeover defense, ownership structure, and performance. This design induces some ambiguity into our analysis, since takeover defenses are evolving during the two-year test period subsequent to the proxy mailing date. Our mailing date is selected to minimize the influence of this problem.

Our sample is based on a group of firms that adopted takeover defenses in 1984 and 1985 and a group of firms that did not adopt takeover defenses during those years. Our intent in choosing this time frame is to obtain a sample of firms characterized by a wide variety of takeover defenses, since this enhances the power of test statistics from cross-sectional analysis. Comment and Schwert (1995) and Bhagat and Jefferis (1991) show that the 1984 and 1985 period contains a substantial amount of information about the status of takeover defenses at the end of 1985, in that many firms that had defenses in place at the end of 1985 adopted them during the 1984 and 1985 period. Using the 1984 and 1985 period as a reference point therefore increases the likelihood of being able to identify firms without takeover defenses. We begin with a group of firms that adopted management-sponsored antitakeover amendments in 1984 and 1985. One source of data is the Jarrell and Poulsen (1987) database. We combine this with a group of firms that enacted antigreenmail charter amendments. Jarrell and Poulsen's data are drawn from Kidder Peabody (1984) and the Securities and Exchange Commission's (SEC's) Office of Tender Offers. The antigreenmail sample was supplied by the New York Stock Exchange. Antigreenmail amendments, which require managers to obtain shareholder approval before a targeted repurchase of an equity stake at a premium to the market price, do not necessarily reduce the likelihood of a takeover. Bhagat and Jefferis (1991) report that these amendments are associated with the adoption of other antitakeover amendments.

This yields a sample of 209 firms. We then eliminate 23 firms for which a copy of the proxy statement cannot be found in the disclosure database. A second sample was constructed by selecting from the Center for Research in Security Prices (CRSP) daily master file that firm closest in total equity value to each firm in the first sample, from the set of all firms having the same three-digit SIC code. For each firm in the second sample, we locate the proxy statement whose mailing date is closest to the mailing date of the corresponding firm in the first sample. Complete proxy documents are available for 176 firms.

After reading each of the 362 proxy statements, we decided to exclude from further analysis firms with a 5 percent blockholder that might be considered to represent affiliated enterprises. The typical blockholder in this group is an officer of a firm holding a minority stake in the excluded firm. The purpose of applying this filter, which results in the elimination of four firms from the amendment sample and 14 firms from the second sample, is to prevent our results from being contaminated by the presence of firms with ownership structure that is qualitatively different from the ownership structure of other firms. The remaining 344 firms comprise the sample used in our analysis.

3.1 Antitakeover Defenses

3.1.1 Sample Construction

The sample construction and the sample period chosen are designed to improve the precision of our model's parameter estimates. If we had randomly sampled from all exchange-listed firms during 1984 or 1985, then the evidence in Comment and Schwert (1995) suggests we would have found that less than 5 percent of our sample had any takeover defense in place in either of these years. Manski and Lerman (1977) and Manski and McFadden (1981) argue that in such a population, appropriate state-based samples provide more efficient parameter estimates compared to a random sample of the same size. Cosslett (1981) finds that a state-based sample of approximately equal proportions is usually a close to optimum design. Manski and Lerman (1977) also propose a correction for the bias introduced by state-based sampling; we utilize their bias correction.

Our sample is based on a group of firms that adopted takeover defenses in 1984 and 1985 and a group of firms matched by industry and size that did not adopt takeover defenses during those years. By considering the period 1984 and 1985 rather than just 1984 or 1985, we were able to approximately double our sample size of adopting firms. Our intent in choosing this time period is to obtain a sample of firms characterized by a wide variety of takeover defenses, since this enhances the power of test statistics from cross-sectional analysis. Comment and Schwert (1995) and Bhagat and Jefferis (1991) show that the 1984 and 1985 period contains a substantial amount of information about the status of takeover defenses at the end of 1985, in that many firms that had defenses in place at the end of 1985 adopted them during the 1984 and 1985 period. Using the 1984 and 1985 period as a reference point therefore increases the likelihood of being able to identify firms without takeover defenses.

We checked the 1987 status of charter amendments for the sample of 196 exchange-listed firms offering antitakeover charter amendments in 1984 and 1985 and a sample of 148 exchange-listed firms that do not offer such charter amendments during the same period. Data are from proxy statements, 10K filings, Investor Responsibility Research Center (1987), and the *Wall Street Journal Index*. Prior to the beginning of 1984, there is no statistically significant difference in the frequency of previously enacted antitakeover amendments between firms that propose amendments and those that do not. There is a statistically significant difference in the frequency of amendments enacted any time before the end of 1987. This suggests that the experience of sample firms in 1984 and 1985 is representative of their overall experience with enactment of antitakeover amendments.

As noted above, while the sample was selected to ensure approximately equal proportions of firms proposing takeover defenses in 1984 and 1985, subsequent analysis of the sample firms (as detailed below) indicated that many of the firms that did not propose a takeover defense in 1984 and 1985 already had takeover defenses in place. Verifying the takeover defense status of the sample firms is rather labor-intensive; we read in detail more than 2,200 proxy statements to verify the takeover defense status of the 344 sample firms—hence the unequal sizes of the takeover defense and nontakeover defense samples. We utilize the Manski and Lerman (1977) state-based sampling bias correction.

3.1.2 Antitakeover Charter Amendments

There is no convenient data source that annually lists the various antitakeover measures that a particular corporation has in place. We consulted four data sources to identify the status of takeover defenses at the 344 firms. From the q data and disclosure databases, we obtained 85 percent or 2,237 of the proxy documents issued by sample firms between 1980 and the end of a two-year period beginning with the proxy mailing date. Table 3.1 notes the number of proxies we sought and were able to find for the sample of 344 NYSE- and AMEX-listed firms for the period 1980 through 1987. Though we were able to access 85 percent of the proxies we sought, it is possible that we might have systematically missed reading the proxies of certain firms, such as small firms. Or we may have missed reading the proxy of a particular firm for several consecutive years. To address these concerns we also provide a correlation matrix of missing proxies. High correlations would have validated such concerns; this appears not to be the case.

The proxy documents provided us with information about the status of takeover defenses. We then incorporated the information in the Linn and McConnell (1983) database, which describes the adoption of takeover defenses at 475 NYSE-listed firms that proposed antitakeover amendments between 1960 and 1980. We also cross-checked our data on charter amendments against the Investor Responsibility Research Center (1987) survey of amendments implemented by Fortune 500 firms through the end of 1987. Finally, we searched the *Wall Street Journal Index* for the year of and two years

Table 3.1
Proxy statements on takeover defenses

Panel A: Number of proxy statements we sought (for information on takeover defenses) and were able to find for the sample of 344 NYSE- and AMEX-listed firms for the period 1980 through 1987

	Year								
	1980	1981	1982	1983	1984	1985	1986	1987	Total
Number sought	344	344	344	344	344	344	341	203	2,608
Number read	227	288	300	301	317	318	305	181	2,237
Number missing	117	56	44	43	27	26	36	22	371

Panel B: Correlation matrix of missing proxy statements between two years in the period 1980 through 1987

	1981	1982	1983	1984	1985	1986	1987
1980	.28	.24	.09	.08	−.00	.05	−.00
1981		.39	.18	.04	.12	.07	.04
1982			.18	.23	.04	.00	.03
1983				.24	.05	.06	.07
1984					−.10	.17	.13
1985						.23	−.10
1986							.17

subsequent to the 1984 and 1985 proxy mailing date for the 344 sample firms. Appendix A[1] provides a list of sample firms, along with the structure of their takeover defenses as of 1986 or 1987. Of the 344 firms in our sample, 207 firms or 60.2 percent of the sample had a fair-price or supermajority amendment in place by the end of 1987. A total of 224 firms or 65.1 percent of the sample had enacted classified board amendments. Table 3.2 notes the frequency distribution of these and other characteristics of our sample firms.

3.1.3 Poison Pills

Information on poison pills was obtained from three sources. Michael Ryngaert provided us with the sample used in Ryngaert (1988), which consists of 380 listed firms that adopted poison pills from 1982 through 1986. We also searched the *Wall Street Journal Index* for the

---

1. Appendix A is available at ⟨http://leeds.colorado.edu/faculty/bhagat⟩.

Table 3.2
Defensive activity, attempted and actual change in control, and management turnover frequencies for 344 NYSE- and AMEX-listed firms from 1980 through 1987

Panel A: Frequency of defensive activity

	Number of Firms
Fair-price or supermajority amendment[a]	207
Classified board amendment[a]	224
Poison pill[b]	210
All three of the above (superdefense)	139
None of the three above (no defense)	69

Panel B: State of incorporation

	Number of Firms
Firms incorporated in Delaware[c]	181
Firms that changed their state of incorporation[c,d]	17

Panel C: Change in corporate control[e]

	Number of Firms
Leveraged buyout (all)	14
Leveraged buyout (pressured)[f]	7
Hostile takeover[g]	12
Nonhostile takeover[h]	22
Attempted change in control[i]	30
No actual or attempted change in control	266

period beginning with the proxy mailing and ending two years subsequent to the proxy mailing. Finally, we identified the existence of a small number of pills using proxy documents. The 210 sample firms (61.1 percent of sample) that had poison pills in place by the end of our test period are described in appendix A.

3.1.4 State of Incorporation

We used *Moody's Manuals*, proxy statements, and the *Wall Street Journal Index* to identify the state of incorporation and changes in the state of incorporation. As of 1987, 181 sample firms were incorporated in Delaware. Seventeen firms changed their state of incorporation between 1980 and 1987; in all but one case, reincorporation resulted in the firm's being incorporated in Delaware.

Table 3.2
(*continued*)

Panel D: Management turnover[j]

	Number of Firms
Partial turnover[k]	174
Complete turnover[l]	37
No turnover	133

a. Information on existence of fair-price, supermajority, and classified board amendments was obtained from proxy statements for the years 1980 through 1987 of sample firms, the Linn and McConnell (1983) dataset, the Investor Responsibility Research Center (1987) survey, and the *Wall Street Journal Index* for 1984 through 1987.

b. Information on poison pills was obtained from Ryngaert's (1988) sample, the *Wall Street Journal Index*, and proxy statements.

c. Data from *Moody's Manuals*, proxy statements, and the *Wall Street Journal Index*.

d. All but one firm reincorporated in Delaware.

e. Information from the *Wall Street Journal Index* starting in 1984 or 1985 through two subsequent years.

f. The LBO occurred in response to an external takeover threat, or the initial offer was rejected.

g. The initial offer was rejected or resisted by target management

h. Target management did not publicly resist the takeover.

i. An attempted change in control that was unsuccessful.

j. Change in the top two officers listed in order in the *Directory of Corporate Affiliations* or *Standard and Poor's Register of Corporations, Directors, and Executives* for 1984 or 1985 through two subsequent years.

k. Change in one of the top two officers.

l. Change in both the top two officers.

3.2 Change in Corporate Control

We use the *Wall Street Journal Index* to identify changes in corporate control or attempted changes in corporate control during the test period. Fourteen of the 344 firms in our sample experienced a leveraged buyout or a management buyout. In seven of these 14 cases, the buyout was either in response to an external takeover threat, or the initial offer was rejected by the firm; we refer to these as pressured LBOs. Twelve firms were taken over following a hostile bid. An offer is defined as hostile if the initial offer was rejected by the target firm's managers or if the managers resisted the offer through lawsuits, search for white knights, and so on. Sometimes the initial hostile bidder was unsuccessful. If the target of a hostile bid was taken over by another bidder (friendly or otherwise) during the two-year test period, the takeover is classified as hostile. Twenty-two sample firms experienced a nonhostile takeover. Thirty sample firms experienced an attempted change in control that was not successful. In some cases, target management actively resisted the offer. In other cases, the bidder ran into regulatory, financial, or other difficulties that led to withdrawal of the bid. In a few cases, no formal offer was received, but newspaper accounts suggested that the firm was a takeover target or that dissident shareholders were attempting some change in control. The remaining 266 sample firms experienced neither a change in control nor an attempted change in control. Appendix B[2] lists the target firms that experienced a change in control or attempted change in control, with a brief description of the control activity.

3.3 Management Turnover

We identified the top two officers at sample firms by consulting the *Directory of Corporate Affiliations* and *Standard and Poor's Register of Corporations, Directors, and Executives.* We track the identity of these individuals during the three-year period beginning with the proxy mailing. This enables us to analyze management turnover in the year of the proxy mailing as well as the two-year period subsequent to the mailing. From these sources, we also obtained the ages of the top two officers in the year of the proxy mailing.

We define management turnover as partial if the identity of one of the top two officers changes during the course of a year. If the identity of both individuals changes, management turnover is said to be complete. When a firm experiences both partial turnover and complete turnover (in different years), we classify turnover as complete. We have 174 cases of partial turnover, 37 cases of complete turnover, and 133 cases of no turnover in our sample of 344 firms. These firms and their turnover classification are noted in appendix C.[3]

We consider the top two officers listed in order in the *Directory* or *Register* rather than individuals with titles of president or chair, since such titles are sometimes retained by figureheads without real executive power. We found that the two officers who signed the proxy statement were often the same as the two officers appearing in the *Directory* or *Register*. Morck, Shleifer, and Vishny (1989) conjecture

---

2. Appendix B is available at ⟨http://leeds.colorado.edu/faculty/bhagat⟩.
3. Appendix C is available at ⟨http://leeds.colorado.edu/faculty/bhagat⟩.

that individuals signing the proxy statement are most likely to be the individuals wielding executive power in the firm. Our data are consistent with this conjecture.

We were unable to identify the names of the top two officers in 22 firm-years. For five firms we had the names for year 1 but none for year 2. For another 12 firms we had the names for year 2 but none for year 3. In each of these 17 cases the firm was involved in either a takeover or an LBO. We classify these 17 firms as cases of complete turnover. In three cases we had no information on management in any year; we classified these observations as no turnover. In two cases we had management information for some but not all of the years; these were also classified as no turnover.

We examine the sensitivity of our results to this classification scheme with an alternative definition of turnover. In the alternative, we track the experience of executives involved in a change in control using the acquiring firm's entry in *National Register Publishing Company: Corporate Affiliations*. When the officer of an acquired firm becomes one of the senior officers of the acquiring firm, we label the observation as "no turnover." In cases where we were able to identify the top two officers for a particular year but not the adjacent years, we searched the *Register*. Officers serving in other corporations in an adjacent year were classified as being involved in turnover.

3.4   Ownership

We calculate the ownership position of different individuals and groups using information reported in the proxy statement. Beneficial ownership includes direct ownership, indirect ownership through family members, trusts, or partnerships, and contingent ownership in the form of stock options that may be exercised within 60 days. Beneficial ownership of officers and directors as a group, corrected to eliminate the double counting of shares owned jointly, is reported in the proxy. The fraction of voting rights held by officers and directors is calculated by subtracting from beneficial ownership those voting rights attributable to contingent ownership and by adding voting rights attached to other securities such as preferred stock. This provides a rough measure of the votes that we might expect the officers and directors to control. The measure is less than exact because of the ambiguity introduced by including indirect ownership.

Ownership statistics discussed below are based on voting rights. We take this position because voting rights rather than beneficial interests represent decision authority in a control contest.

3.5 Block Ownership

Ownership by 5 percent blockholders is reported in the proxy statement. Institutional investors are required by SEC regulations to report shares as beneficially owned when those shares are held for clients who control the attached voting rights. Mean beneficial ownership is roughly double mean voting power for institutional blockholders in our sample. In contrast, the difference between beneficial ownership and voting rights is less than 2 percent for chief executives. (The mean beneficial ownership for CEOs is 3.50 percent, and their mean voting power is 3.43 percent. The mean beneficial ownership for institutional blockholders is 5.31 percent, whereas their mean voting power is only 2.62 percent.) The block ownership variables in our analysis pertain to those shares for which a blockholder actually controls the voting rights.

We consider the influence of ownership by four groups of blockholders. Independent directors are defined to be directors who are not also officers of the corporation. Affiliated investment plans include employee stock ownership plans (ESOPs), payroll stock ownership plans, and all other affiliated investment plans. We refer to these generically as ESOPs. We also consider block ownership by corporate officers and block ownership by institutions.

We obtained data on institutional ownership from the *Standard & Poor's Stock Guide* during the month preceding the proxy mailing. This statistic is based on beneficial ownership rather than voting rights.

3.6 Firm Performance

We evaluate firm performance using stock returns and variables based on cash flow. Morck, Shleifer, and Vishny (1989), Martin and McConnell (1991), and Palepu (1986) report that stock returns are correlated with managerial turnover and takeover activity. Weisbach (1988) and Murphy and Zimmerman (1993) find that accounting earnings have predictive content. We have explored a wide variety of definitions for stock-market performance and find that our results are somewhat sensitive to the construction of this performance measure. The construction of our performance measures is described in appendix D.[4]

A detailed analysis of the predictive content of different measures of stock-market performance is described in appendix E.[5] Here, we present results based on market-adjusted returns calculated over the 200 trading days preceding the proxy mailing, using the CRSP equal-weighted index as the market proxy. Inference based on this definition of stock-market performance is stronger than but not inconsistent with inference suggested by other measures of stock-market performance. Results based on cash flow are much more robust to variations in specification of how the performance measure is constructed. Our cash-flow return measure is earnings before interest and taxes standardized by the book value of the firm's assets, as in Weisbach (1988). We consider both the level of this variable and its growth rate. These data are obtained from COMPUSTAT (the annual full-coverage file, the primary-supplementary-tertiary file, and the research file). We construct a nine-year series of this variable for each firm in the sample, centered on the year of the proxy mailing. We also constructed an index for industry groups. Our cross-sectional results are not sensitive to the definition of this measure.

3.7 Firm Size

Firm size is represented by the book value of the firm's assets in the year prior to the proxy mailing. These data are from COMPUSTAT.

---

4. Appendix D is available at ⟨http://leeds.colorado.edu/faculty/bhagat⟩.
5. Appendix E is available at ⟨http://leeds.colorado.edu/faculty/bhagat⟩.

4

Joint Distribution of Takeover Activity, Managerial Turnover, and Takeover Defense

4.1 Nonparametric Tests for Independence

We use nonparametric tests to examine the joint distribution of managerial turnover, takeover activity, and takeover defense. These are all categorical variables. Pairwise analysis of their joint distributions leads to three sets of tests. In each test, the null hypothesis is that the frequency of an event such as managerial turnover is uncorrelated with the frequency of a second event, like takeover activity or takeover defense. The alternative hypothesis is that the conditional probability of the first event varies with the frequency of the second event. Tests are distinguished by both the pair of variables being examined and the specification of an event.

Our categorical variables are polychotomous. Suppose that the potential outcomes for variable 1 and variable 2 are

$$v_1 = \{v_{11}, v_{12}, \ldots, v_{1n_1}\}$$
$$v_2 = \{v_{21}, v_{22}, \ldots, v_{2n_2}\}. \tag{4.1}$$

Let v_{i1} be a null event, such as no takeover activity, no takeover defense, or no managerial turnover. All other realizations of v_i correspond to some type of activity. For each pairwise relationship, we report three tests concerning the joint distribution of two categorical variables. One null hypothesis is

$$Pr(v_{1k}|v_{21}) = Pr(v_{1k}|v_{2j}) \quad \forall\, k. \tag{4.2}$$

The test is based on a $2 \times n_1$ contingency table. Under the null, the likelihood of *every* event in v_1 is invariant with respect to the realization $v_2 = v_{21}$ or $v_2 = v_{2j}$. If v_1 represents takeover activity and v_2 denotes takeover defense, the null hypothesis is that the distribution

of takeover activity given no defense is the same as the distribution
of takeover activity given defense j. The hypothesis concerns all
types of takeover activity and one type of takeover defense.

A second hypothesis of interest is

$$Pr(v_{1k}|v_{21}) = Pr(v_{1k}|v_{2j}) \quad \forall\, k, \forall\, j. \tag{4.3}$$

This is associated with an $n_1 \times n_2$ contingency table that represents
the joint distribution of v_1 and v_2. In the context of our example, the
null hypothesis is that the conditional distribution of takeover activity is the same for all realizations of takeover defense (including
no defense). This test is distinguished from the test described in the
previous paragraph in that the second test concerns all realizations
of the variable v_2, whereas the first test concerns two realizations of
that variable.

A final hypothesis focuses on a particular realization of v_1. The
null hypothesis is

$$Pr(v_{1k}|v_{21}) = Pr(v_{1k}|v_{2j}) \quad j \neq 1. \tag{4.4}$$

This test is distinguished from the first test in that it focuses on a
particular event in v_1 rather than all events in v_1. For example, we
test whether the frequency of hostile takeovers is correlated with the
presence of poison pills. The test is associated with a 2×2 contingency table. The rows of the table correspond to the frequency of
the events v_{1j} and $U_{k \neq j} v_{1k}$. The columns of the table correspond to
$v_2 = v_{21}$ and $v_2 = v_{2j}$.

Our hypothesis tests exploit the Pearson χ^2 statistic and an alternative known as the Yates corrected statistic. These are described in
Bishop, Feinberg, and Holland (1976). Both statistics have an asymptotic distribution that is $\chi^2(q)$, where the degrees of freedom q depend
on the dimensions of the contingency table. The Yates correction is
appropriate when event frequencies are low, since its finite sample
distribution more closely resembles the asymptotic distribution than
does the distribution of the Pearson statistic in this situation.

4.2 The Joint Distribution of Takeover Activity and Managerial Turnover

Table 4.1 describes the joint distribution of management turnover
and takeover activity. The data reveal a strong positive correlation
between these variables that is consistent with evidence presented

Table 4.1
Joint distribution of management turnover and takeover activity between 1984 and 1987 in a sample of 344 NYSE-listed and AMEX-listed firms

Cell entries denote the conditional frequency of management turnover given takeover activity. Where appropriate, the χ^2 statistic that is used to test the null hypothesis of conditional independence of management turnover given takeover activity is reported in brackets.

	Management Turnover		
Takeover Activity	No Turnover[a] (n = 133)	Partial Turnover[b] (n = 174)	Complete Turnover[c] (n = 37)
Full sample (n = 344)[d]	0.39	0.51	0.11
No activity (n = 266)[e]	0.43	0.53	0.04
Attempted (n = 30)[f]	0.33	0.57	0.10
	[0.65]	[0.03]	[0.96]
Leveraged buyout	0.29	0.50	0.21**
(n = 14)[†]	[0.60]	[0.00]	[5.12]
Nonhostile (n = 22)[g†]	0.18**	0.18*	0.64*
	[4.15]	[8.51]	[83.39]
Hostile (n = 12)[h†]	0.08**	0.42	0.50*
	[4.31]	[0.22]	[34.46]

a. Firms where neither partial nor complete turnover occurred.
b. Firms where one of the top two officers changed.
c. Firms where both of the top two officers changed.
d. The Pearson χ^2 statistic of 99.04, which is distributed as $\chi^2(8)$ asymptotically, rejects at 1 percent the null hypothesis of independence for the conditional distribution of takeover activity and management turnover.
e. Firms where no actual or attempted change in control occurred.
f. Firms where an attempted change in control was unsuccessful.
g. Firms where the target management did not publicly resist the takeover.
h. Firms where the target management resisted or rejected the initial offer.
* Indicates that the Yates χ^2 statistic, which is distributed as $\chi^2(1)$ asymptotically, rejects at 1 percent the null hypothesis of independence for the conditional distribution of management turnover with respect to control activity. This test is based on a 2×2 contingency table. The turnover variable has a value of 1 if the specified type of turnover occurs and 0 otherwise. The takeover activity variable is equal to 0 when there is no control activity and equal to 1 when the specified type of takeover activity occurs.
** Indicates that this same statistic rejects the null at 5 percent. The distribution of the Yates statistic more closely resembles χ^2 than does the distribution of more familiar Pearson statistic when the event of interest occurs with low frequency in finite samples. The Yates statistic has a smaller size than the Pearson statistic and is therefore associated with less frequent rejection of the null.
† Indicates that the Pearson χ^2 statistic, which is distributed as $\chi^2(2)$ asymptotically, rejects at 1 percent the null hypothesis of independence for the conditional distribution of management turnover with respect to takeover activity. Under the null, the conditional distribution of management turnover given no control activity is equal to the conditional distribution of management turnover given the specified type of control activity.

by Martin and McConnell (1991). In the first column of the table, we see that the frequency of no management turnover decreases monotonically as we move from firms that experience no form of takeover activity through firms that experience an attempted takeover to firms that are taken over by outsiders. The evidence in the last column of the table indicates that the frequency of complete management turnover at firms involved in completed takeovers exceeds the frequency of complete management turnover at firms that experience attempted takeovers and the frequency of complete turnover at firms that experience no takeover activity. Hostile takeovers represent the only departure from monotonicity in this column. A recent paper by Comment and Schwert (1997) notes that the hostile/nonhostile definition we employ (which is employed by other authors, as well) is not very useful in distinguishing between these takeovers in economic terms. Hence, our similar results for complete turnover for hostile and nonhostile takeovers is consistent with the Comment and Schwert (1997) conclusions.

The contrast between the distribution of turnover at firms that experience no takeover activity and the distribution of turnover at firms involved in either a nonhostile takeover or a hostile takeover is especially sharp. We observe substantial differences in all three measures of turnover. (These are not independent.) At firms that experience no takeover activity, partial turnover is more common than complete turnover. Complete turnover is prevalent at firms taken over by outsiders, both in the case where the takeover is hostile and in the case where the takeover is nonhostile. For example, 64 percent (50 percent) of companies in the nonhostile (hostile) takeover subsample experienced complete management turnover—compared to 4 percent of the companies that experienced no takeover activity. Also, 18 percent (8 percent) of companies in the nonhostile (hostile) takeover subsample experienced no management turnover—compared to 43 percent of the companies that experienced no takeover activity.

The positive correlation between management turnover and takeover activity is statistically significant by a number of measures. A χ^2 test rejects at 1 percent the null hypothesis that the distribution of management turnover given no takeover activity is the same as the distribution of management turnover given an LBO, nonhostile takeover or hostile takeover. (These are three separate tests.) A joint test for conditional independence that incorporates all five categories of the takeover activity variable also rejects the null at 1 percent. In the individual cells, we observe statistically significant differences between turnover measures at firms that experience no takeover activity and turnover measures at firms that are taken over by outsiders.

In short, the evidence reported in table 4.1 indicates that takeover activity is associated with an increase in management turnover in our data. This suggests that our taxonomy of takeover activity and management turnover is meaningful. Results reported below concerning the effect of defensive activity on takeovers and managerial turnover should not be attributed to measurement error in these variables or some sort of sampling anomaly.

4.3 The Joint Distribution of Takeover Activity and Takeover Defense

Table 4.2 describes the joint distribution of takeover activity and takeover defense. The contrast between the experience of firms that have takeover defenses and the experience of firms that do not have takeover defenses is in general quite strong. Defenses are associated with less frequent takeover activity, as reported by Pound (1987). The data in the first column of the table reveal that 70 percent of the firms have no takeover defense experience no type of takeover activity, while 85 percent of the firms that have a fair-price provision, a classified board, and a poison pill enjoy a similar experience. The difference is statistically significant at 1 percent. Similar differences are observed in the case of individual takeover defenses. Among the defenses that we consider, only incorporation in the state of Delaware does not seem to be related to the subsequent takeover experience of firms.

Much of the variation in takeover activity reflected in column 1 is attributable to the correlation between takeover defense and the frequency of nonhostile takeovers. Nineteen percent of the firms that have no takeover defense are involved in a nonhostile takeover during our test period. At firms that have at least one major takeover defense (that is, a fair-price provision, a classified board, or a poison pill), no more than 3 percent of the sample is involved in a nonhostile takeover. The frequency of nonhostile takeovers is 1 percent at firms that have a fair-price provision, a classified board, and a poison pill.

Table 4.2
Joint distribution of takeover activity and takeover defense between 1984 and 1987 for
a sample of 344 NYSE-listed and AMEX-listed firms.

Cell entries denote the conditional frequency of takeover activity given takeover defense. Where appropriate, the χ^2 statistic that is used to test the null hypothesis of
conditional independence of takeover activity given takeover defense is reported in
brackets.

Takeover Defense[a]	Takeover Activity				
	None[b] (n = 266)	Attempted[c] (n = 30)	Leveraged Buyout (n = 14)	Nonhostile[d] (n = 22)	Hostile[e] (n = 12)
Full sample (n = 344)[f]	0.77	0.09	0.04	0.06	0.04
No defense (n = 69)[g]	0.70	0.02	0.09	0.19	0.02
Fair price, classified board, and poison pill (n = 139)	0.85* [5.80]	0.07 [1.56]	0.04 [0.92]	0.01* [18.34]	0.01 [0.02]
Fair price (n = 207)	0.82** [4.31]	0.09 [3.02]	0.03 [0.13]	0.02* [21.10]	0.04 [0.31]
Classify board (n = 224)	0.81** [3.85]	0.09 [3.00]	0.04 [2.11]	0.03* [18.48]	0.04 [0.23]
Poison pill (n = 210)	0.81 [2.97]	0.10** [4.11]	0.03 [2.96]	0.03* [18.46]	0.03 [0.16]
Delaware (n = 181)	0.76 [0.02]	0.11 [1.59]	0.03 [0.78]	0.07 [1.18]	0.03 [0.00]

The difference between the frequency of nonhostile takeovers at
firms that have defenses and the frequency of nonhostile takeovers
at firms that have some type of defense rejects the null at 1 percent in
every case but Delaware. We also reject at 1 percent for every defense but Delaware the hypothesis that the distribution of takeover
activity is independent of the presence of takeover defense. Finally,
we are able to reject at 1 percent the null of independence for the
joint distribution of takeover activity and takeover defense.

The data in table 4.2 reveal an additional disparity in the experience of firms that have takeover defenses and the experience of firms
that do not have takeover defenses. At firms without defenses, 94
percent of takeover attempts result in some sort of completed transaction. Roughly 50 percent of attempted takeovers are successful at

Table 4.2
(*continued*)

a. The Pearson χ^2 statistic rejects at 1 percent the null hypothesis of independence for the conditional distribution of takeover activity given takeover defense for every defense but Delaware. The null hypothesis is that the distribution of takeover activity given the specified takeover defense is the same as the distribution of takeover activity given no takeover defense. The test statistic is distributed as $\chi^2(4)$.
b. Firms where no actual or attempted change in control occurred.
c. Firms where an attempted change in control was unsuccessful.
d. The target management did not publicly resist the takeover.
e. The target management resisted or rejected the initial offer.
f. The Pearson χ^2 statistic of 42.73 rejects at 1 percent the null hypothesis of independence for the joint distribution of takeover activity and takeover defense. The null hypothesis is that the conditional distribution of takeover activity given takeover defense is independent of the status of the firms with respect to takeover defense. The takeover defense variable has a value of 0 if a firm has no takeover defense, a value of 2 if the firm has a fair price provision, a classified board and a poison pill, and a value of 1 otherwise. The test statistic is distributed as $\chi^2(8)$.
g. Firms where none of the following types of takeover defenses occurred: fair-price provision, classified board, and poison pill.
* Indicates that the χ^2 statistic rejects at 1 percent the null hypothesis of independence for the conditional independence of takeover activity given takeover defense at 1 percent. This test is based on a 2×2 contingency table. The change in takeover variable has a value of 1 if the specified control event occurs and 0 otherwise. The takeover defense variable assumes a value of 1 if the given type of takeover defense is present and a value of 0 if *no defense* is present.
** Indicates that this same statistic rejects the null at 5 percent. We report the Yates corrected χ^2 value for all categories other than None. For the category None, we report Pearson statistics. Both statistics are distributed as $\chi^2(1)$ asymptotically. The distribution of the Yates statistic more closely resembles χ^2 than does the Pearson statistic when the event of interest occurs with low frequency in finite samples. The Yates statistic has a smaller size than the Pearson statistic and is therefore associated with less frequent rejection of the null.

firms with some sort of takeover defense. A χ^2 test rejects at 1 percent the null hypothesis that the probability of a completed offer, given an attempt, is the same for firms with no defenses and firms with a fair-price amendment, classified board, and poison pill. The same test rejects the null at 1 percent for all of the individual defenses, including incorporation in Delaware.

In sum, the evidence in table 4.2 indicates that takeover defenses are associated with both a decrease in the frequency of completed transactions and a decrease in the frequency of successful attempts among firms that are takeover targets. These differences are statistically significant, especially in the case of nonhostile takeovers.

4.4   The Joint Distribution of Management Turnover and Takeover Defense

The joint distribution of management turnover and takeover defense is described in table 4.3. In the first column of the table, we see that the overall frequency of no management turnover is insensitive to the presence of takeover defense. Roughly 39 percent of the firms in the sample experience no management turnover during the test period. This statement applies to firms that have no takeover defenses, to firms that have some takeover defenses, and to firms that have comprehensive takeover defenses.

There is nonetheless a strong relationship between the presence of takeover defenses and the pattern of management turnover. In the second and third columns of the table, we see that firms that have takeover defenses experience complete management turnover less frequently than firms without takeover defenses and partial turnover more frequently than firms without takeover defenses. The pattern is consistent across the different types of defense. For example, 6 percent of firms that have all three types of defenses (fair price, classified board, and poison pill) experience complete management turnover compared to 23 percent of the firms that have no defenses.

The difference between the frequency of partial turnover at firms that have all three defenses and the frequency of partial turnover at firms that have only one type of defense rejects at 1 percent the null hypothesis that the frequency of partial turnover is independent of takeover defense, in every case but Delaware. Similar results obtain for complete management turnover. We reject at 1 percent for every defense but Delaware the hypothesis that the distribution of management turnover is independent of the presence of takeover defense. Finally, we are able to reject at 1 percent the null of independence for the joint distribution of management turnover and takeover defense.

Collectively, the evidence in table 4.3 indicates that the presence of takeover defenses is uncorrelated with the frequency of no management turnover but strongly correlated with the frequency of complete management turnover. Given our definitions of no, partial, and complete turnovers, one could restate the above results as follows: The presence of takeover defenses is uncorrelated with the frequency of CEO departures but strongly correlated with the identity of the new CEO. At firms that have takeover defenses, a departing CEO tends to be replaced by a subordinate. At firms without takeover

Table 4.3
Joint distribution of management turnover and takeover defense between 1984 and 1987 in a sample of 344 NYSE-listed and AMEX-listed firms

Cell entries denote the conditional frequency of management turnover given takeover defense. Where appropriate, the χ^2 statistic that is used to test the null hypothesis of conditional independence of management turnover given takeover defense is reported in brackets.

Takeover Defense[a]	Management Turnover		
	No Turnover[b] (n = 133)	Partial Turnover[c] (n = 174)	Complete Turnover[d] (n = 37)
Full sample (n = 344)[e]	0.39	0.51	0.11
No defense (n = 69)	0.42	0.35	0.23
Fair price, classified board, and poison pill (n = 139)	0.39 [0.19]	0.55* [7.85]	0.06* [13.73]
Fair price (n = 207)	0.39 [0.15]	0.53* [7.17]	0.08* [12.80]
Classify board (n = 224)	0.38 [0.17]	0.55* [7.67]	0.07* [14.35]
Poison pill (n = 210)	0.36 [0.75]	0.58* [10.85]	0.06* [16.11]
Delaware (n = 181)	0.39 [0.05]	0.49 [0.43]	0.12 [0.45]

a. The Pearson χ^2 statistic rejects at 1 percent the null hypothesis of independence for the conditional distribution of management turnover given takeover defense for every defense but Delaware. The null hypothesis is that the frequency of management turnover given the specified takeover defense is the same as the distribution of takeover activity given no takeover defense. The test statistic is distributed as $\chi^2(2)$.
b. Firms where neither partial nor complete turnover occurred.
c. Firms where one of the top two officers changed.
d. Firms where both of the top two officers changed.
e. The Pearson χ^2 statistic of 17.95 rejects at 1 percent the null hypothesis of independence for the joint distribution of management turnover and takeover defense. The null hypothesis is that the conditional distribution of management turnover given takeover defense is independent of the status of the firms with respect to takeover defense. The takeover defense variable has a value of 0 if a firm has no takeover defense, a value of 2 if the firm has a fair-price provision, a classified board, and a poison pill, and a value of 1 otherwise. The test statistic is distributed as $\chi^2(4)$.
* Indicates that the Pearson χ^2 statistic, which is distributed as $\chi^2(1)$ asymptotically, rejects at 1 percent the null hypothesis of independence for the conditional independence of management turnover given takeover defense. This test is based on a 2 × 2 contingency table. The change in takeover variable has a value of 1 if the specified type of management turnover occurs and 0 otherwise. The takeover defense variable assumes a value of 1 if the given type of takeover defense is present and a value of 0 if *no defense* is present.
** Indicates that this same statistic rejects the null at 5 percent.

defenses, it is much more likely that both the CEO and his subordinate depart simultaneously.

These data, the data in table 4.1, and the data in table 4.2 are jointly consistent with evidence presented by Morck, Shleifer, and Vishny (1989). These authors report that complete managerial turnover is associated with takeover activity. In contrast, replacement of the CEO by the current board of directors is associated with the promotion of an internal candidate.

5

Bootstrap Regression Results

5.1 Performance and Takeover Activity

Table 5.1 describes the relationship between performance and take-over activity and the relationship between performance and management turnover, both as a function of takeover defense. The estimates presented in the table are obtained by regressing performance measures on a set of interactive dummies. In panel A, where we focus on takeover activity, the dummy variables represent the status of takeover defenses at firms that are not takeover targets. The intercept describes mean performance at firms involved in a takeover, buyout, or attempted takeover. Slope coefficients represent the difference in performance between firms that are not takeover targets and firms that are takeover targets, as a function of takeover defense. A positive coefficient implies that firms that are not takeover targets exhibit superior performance relative to firms that are takeover targets.

We estimate two versions of this model. The relationship between performance and takeover activity is allowed to vary with takeover defense in the unconstrained model. Here, the interactive dummies that represent the joint status of the firm with respect to takeover defense and takeover activity are labeled β_1, β_2, and β_3. The variable associated with β_1 has a value of 1 if a firm has no takeover defense and experiences no takeover activity and a value of 0 otherwise. The variable associated with β_2 (β_3) has a value of 1 if a firm has a poison pill (other defense) and experiences no takeover activity and a value of 0 otherwise.

In the constrained model, the slope coefficient that represents the relationship between performance and takeover activity is independent of takeover defense. The t-statistic for this slope coefficient is a test of the joint hypothesis $\beta_1 = \beta_2 = \beta_3 = 0$ against the alternative

Table 5.1
Performance versus takeover activity and management turnover

Bootstrap regression results of performance measures on dummy variables that represent the joint experience of firms with (1) takeover activity and takeover defense and (2) management turnover and takeover defense.

Panel A: Performance versus takeover activity

Performance Measure	Nobs	Const	Unconstrained Model: Interactive Dummy for No Takeover Activity[a] and Takeover Defense[b]					Constrained Model: Dummy for No Takeover Activity[a]	
			No Defense[c] β_1	Poison Pill β_2	Other Defense[d] β_3	Test[e] $\beta_1=\beta_2$	Test[f] $\beta_1=\beta_2=\beta_3$	Const	Dummy[g]
Market-adjusted stock returns for 200 trading days preceding test period	303	-3.06	7.11	22.70	0.26	1.48	2.69	-3.31	15.64
		-0.34	0.50	2.14	0.02			-0.34	1.36
Cash flow based return on assets, years -4 through -1	312	46.43	3.79	8.99	6.72	1.54	2.09	46.50	7.69‡
		10.57	0.69	2.49	1.41			10.23	2.14
Growth in cash flow based return on assets, years -4 through -1	312	-2.29	-2.13	0.40	-0.63	1.91‡	2.83	-2.33	-0.21
		-2.38	-0.59	0.38	-0.46			-2.30	-0.17

Panel B: Performance versus management turnover

Performance Measure	Nobs	Const	Unconstrained Model: Interactive Dummy for No Management Turnover and Takeover Defense[h]					Constrained Model: Dummy for No Management Turnover	
			No Defense[c] β_1	Poison Pill β_2	Other Defense[d] β_3	Test[e] $\beta_1=\beta_2$	Test[f] $\beta_1=\beta_2=\beta_3$	Const	Dummy[g]
Market-adjusted stock returns for 200 trading days preceding test period	303	2.04	-12.08	34.05	6.28	2.98†	5.58†	2.07	18.20†
		0.39	-0.96	3.39	0.37			0.40	2.31
Cash flow based return on assets, years -4 through -1	312	50.99	3.68	6.39	1.32	1.04	1.25	51.07	4.54
		12.80	0.73	1.70	0.25			12.45	1.48

Table 5.1
(*continued*)

Growth in cash flow based return on assets, years −4 through −1	312	−3.21 −3.86	1.33 2.31	2.39 0.50	1.00 0.54	0.95	1.28	−3.29 −3.89	1.97‡ 1.73

Note: Each set of estimates is based on 200 bootstrap replications of the sample, weighted to correct for sample-selection bias. *T*-statistics based on the bootstrap estimate of the parameter covariance matrix are noted below the coefficients. The sample consists of 344 NYSE- and AMEX-listed firms. The test period is 1984 through 1987. The number of observations varies because of missing financial data.

a. Firms where no actual or attempted change in control occurred.

b. Dummy variables have a value of 1 if the firm experienced no takeover activity and had the specified type of takeover defense. The takeover defense categories are mutually exclusive and collectively exhaustive. A positive coefficient indicates that firms that experienced no takeover activity and had the specified type of takeover defense exhibit positive performance relative to the set of firms that experienced some type of takeover activity. The omitted category is firms that experienced either an attempted takeover or a completed takeover. The performance of this group is represented by the intercept term. β_1, β_2, and β_3 are the coefficients associated with no defense, poison pill, and other defense, respectively.

c. Firms that did not have a fair-price provision, classified board amendment, or poison pill.

d. Firms that had a fair-price provision or classified board amendment but no poison pill.

e. The test statistic, which is based on the difference $\beta_1 - \beta_2$, has a *t*-distribution. We report its absolute value.

f. The test statistic, which is distributed as $F(2, N-4)$ under the null, is calculated using the bootstrap estimate of the parameter covariance matrix. Amemiya (1985) discusses this statistic and its distribution.

g. The *t*-statistic in the constrained regression is a test of the null hypothesis $\beta_1 = \beta_2 = \beta_3 = 0$ against the alternative $\beta_1 = \beta_2 = \beta_3 = k \neq 0$.

h. Dummy variables have a value of 1 if the firm experienced no management turnover and had the specified type of takeover defense. The takeover defense categories are mutually exclusive and collectively exhaustive. A positive slope coefficient indicates that firms that experienced no management turnover and had the specified type of takeover defense exhibit positive performance relative to the set of firms that experience some management turnover. The omitted category is firms that experienced either partial management turnover or complete management turnover. The performance of this group is captured in the intercept term.

† Indicates that the null is rejected at 1 percent.

‡ Indicates that the null is rejected at 5 percent.

$\beta_1 = \beta_2 = \beta_3 = k > 0$. A rejection implies that performance is related to takeover activity, under the maintained hypothesis that takeover defenses do not affect the relationship between performance and takeover activity.

We test the constraint $\beta_1 = \beta_2 = \beta_3$ against the alternative that the relationship between performance and takeover activity varies with takeover defense. The test statistic has an F distribution. We also present a test of the hypothesis $\beta_1 = \beta_2$, which implies that among firms that are not takeover targets, performance at firms that have no takeover defense is the same as performance at firms that have poison pills. In either case, a rejection of the null suggests that the correlation between takeover defense and takeover activity may be performance related.

Consider first the results for the constrained model in panel A. The slope coefficient associated with the absence of takeover activity is positive for two of the three performance measures. This indicates that firms that are not taken over outperform firms that are taken over during the four-year period preceding the test period and is consistent with the performance-based explanation of takeover activity, as noted by Palepu (1986), Morck, Shleifer, and Vishny (1989), Martin and McConnell (1991), and Denis and Serrano (1996). However, the estimated slope coefficients are significantly different from zero for only cash flow based return on assets.

In the unconstrained model, the estimate of β_2 indicates that firms with poison pills that are not taken over outperform takeover targets when either cash-flow or stock-market return is used to measure performance. The F-test rejects the null $\beta_1 = \beta_2 = \beta_3$ at 10 percent when stock-market return is used to measure performance. The t-statistic for $\beta_1 = \beta_2$ rejects the null at 10 percent only in the case where cash-flow growth is used to represent performance.

5.2   Performance and Management Turnover

The relationship between performance and management turnover is described in table 5.1, panel B. The results here are qualitatively similar to those reported in panel A. In the constrained model, the slope coefficients associated with all three performance measures are positive, indicating that firms that do not experience management turnover outperform those that do experience management turnover. (When cash-flow-based ROA is used to represent performance, the model rejects the null at 5 percent. The estimate associated with stock-market return rejects the null at 1 percent.) These findings are consistent with those in Warner, Watts, and Wruck (1988), Weisbach (1988), and Denis and Denis (1995).

The pattern of the estimates from the unconstrained model is similar to the pattern observed in panel A. The estimates of β_2 indicate that managers who enjoy the protection of poison pills outperform managers who subsequently depart from their firms for every performance measure. When stock-market return is used to measure performance, the null is rejected at 1 percent. Neither managers who operate without the protection of takeover defenses nor managers who are shielded by defenses other than poison pills outperform (by a statistically significant margin) managers who are about to depart.

The difference in performance among managers who do not experience turnover is statistically significant only when stock-market return is used as a performance measure. For this measure of performance, we reject at 1 percent both the hypothesis $\beta_1 = \beta_2 = \beta_3$ and the hypothesis $\beta_1 = \beta_2$.

We draw two conclusions from the evidence in table 5.1. First, the cross-sectional relationship between performance and turnover and the cross-sectional relationship between performance and takeovers that we observe in our data are consistent with the hypothesis that takeovers and management turnover are performance related. Thus our data are consistent with previously reported results. Second, it appears that these relationships vary with the status of takeover defenses. The evidence presented in table 5.1 is consistent with the hypothesis that takeover defense affects the relationship between performance and corporate control and also is consistent with the hypothesis that takeover defenses are correlated with some characteristic of firms that covaries with control activity.

5.3   Ownership and Takeover Activity

Table 5.2 describes the relationship between ownership structure and takeover activity and the relationship between ownership structure and management turnover, both as a function of takeover defense. The estimated slope coefficients presented in the table are obtained by regressing ownership variables on the same set of interactive dummies used in the performance regressions. In panel A, the estimates represent the difference in ownership between firms that

Table 5.2
Ownership versus takeover activity and management turnover

Bootstrap regression results of ownership on dummy variables that represent the joint experience of firms with (1), takeover activity and takeover defense and (2) management turnover and takeover defense.

Panel A: Ownership versus takeover activity

Ownership		Unconstrained Model: Interactive Dummies for No Takeover Activity[a] and Takeover Defense[b]						Constrained Model: Dummy for No Takeover Activity[a]	
	Const	No Defense[c] β_1	Poison Pill β_2	Other Defense[d] β_3	Test[e] $\beta_1 = \beta_2$	Test[f] $\beta_1 = \beta_2 = \beta_3$		Const	Dummy[g]
Chief executive officer	4.79	5.00	-2.40	1.37	4.89†	13.15†		4.79	-0.38
	3.28	2.06	-1.61	0.63				3.28	-0.25
Directors and officers	10.66	9.09	-3.22	3.80	5.63†	18.21†		10.66	0.27
	5.15	2.73	-1.50	1.28				5.15	0.13
Institutions	42.00	-14.20	-0.01	-11.29	5.03†	16.71†		42.00	-4.66†
	11.72	-4.25	-0.00	-3.71				11.72	-2.02
Block ownership by officers	5.94	9.62	-1.82	2.54	5.67†	16.17†		5.94	1.05
	3.36	3.15	-0.98	1.14				3.36	0.58
Block ownership by directors	2.86	-0.12	-1.98	-1.23	2.05‡	2.69		2.86	-1.50
	2.61	-0.07	-1.76	-0.95				2.61	-1.36
Block ownership by institutions	3.18	-0.10	-0.82	-0.76	1.34	1.48		3.18	-0.68
	4.48	-0.09	-1.02	-0.83				4.48	-0.89
Block ownership by ESOPs	1.77	-1.64	-0.10	-0.62	1.46	2.69		1.77	-0.47
	3.68	-3.28	-0.15	-1.04				3.68	-0.85

Panel B: Ownership versus management turnover

Ownership	Unconstrained Model: Interactive Dummies for No Management Turnover and Takeover Defense[h]						Constrained Model: Dummy for No Management Turnover	
	Const	No Defense[c] β_1	Poison Pill β_2	Other Defense[d] β_3	Test[e] $\beta_1 = \beta_2$	Test[f] $\beta_1 = \beta_2 = \beta_3$	Const	Dummy[g]
Chief executive officer	3.49	9.44	0.38	2.32	4.61[†]	10.79[†]	3.49	2.74[†]
	5.30	2.54	0.40	1.24			5.30	2.21
Directors and officers	8.90	16.07	0.74	4.68	5.27[†]	15.04[†]	8.90	4.90[†]
	8.48	3.79	0.53	1.34			8.48	2.83
Institutions	41.68	−14.36	−4.12	−12.21	2.83[†]	5.33[†]	41.68	−8.08[†]
	12.92	−3.11	−1.48	−3.99			12.92	−3.22
Block ownership by officers	5.33	15.43	0.24	1.78	5.71[†]	16.70[†]	5.33	3.90[†]
	5.78	2.98	0.17	0.77			5.78	2.29
Block ownership by directors	1.92	0.15	−1.07	0.37	1.45	1.60	1.92	−0.50
	3.79	0.10	−1.76	0.30			3.79	−0.82
Block ownership by institutions	2.94	−1.07	−0.35	−1.55	1.28	1.44	2.94	−0.76
	6.81	−0.93	−0.44	−2.48			6.81	−1.23
Block ownership by ESOPs	1.33	−0.53	0.41	0.40	1.26	1.24	1.33	0.20
	4.20	−0.75	0.59	0.63			4.20	0.40

Note: Each set of estimates is based on 200 bootstrap replications of the sample, weighted to correct for sample-selection bias. *T*-statistics based on the bootstrap estimate of the parameter covariance matrix are noted below the coefficients. All regressions use the full sample of 344 NYSE- and AMEX-listed firms. The test period is 1984 through 1987.

Table 5.2
(*continued*)

a. Firms where no actual or attempted change in control occurred.

b. Dummy variables have a value of 1 if the firm experienced no takeover activity and had the specified type of takeover defense. The takeover defense categories are mutually exclusive and collectively exhaustive. A positive slope coefficient indicates that firms that experienced no takeover activity and had the specified type of takeover defense exhibited ownership in excess of that observed at firms that experienced some type of takeover activity. The omitted category is firms that experienced either an attempted takeover or a completed takeover. Mean ownership for this group is represented by the intercept term. β_1, β_2, and β_3 are the coefficients associated with no defense, poison pill, and other defense, respectively.

c. Firms that did not have a fair-price provision, classified board amendment, or poison pill.

d. Firms that had a fair-price provision or classified board amendment but no poison pill.

e. The test statistic, which is based on the difference $\beta_1 - \beta_2$ has a t-distribution. We report its absolute value.

f. The test statistic, which is distributed as F(2,340) under the null $\beta_1 = \beta_2 = \beta_3$, is calculated using the bootstrap estimate of the parameter covariance matrix. Amemiya (1985) discusses the statistic and its distribution.

g. The t-statistic in the constrained regression is a test of the null hypothesis $\beta_1 = \beta_2 = \beta_3 = 0$ against the alternative $\beta_1 = \beta_2 = \beta_3 = k \neq 0$.

h. Dummy variables have a value of 1 if the firm experienced no management turnover and had the specified type of takeover defense. The takeover defense categories are mutually exclusive and collectively exhaustive. A positive slope coefficient indicates that firms that experienced no management turnover and had the specified type of takeover defense had ownership of the specified type in excess of that at firms that experienced some management turnover. The omitted category is firms that experienced either partial management turnover or complete management turnover. The ownership structure of this group is captured in the intercept term.

† Indicates that the null is rejected at 1 percent.

‡ Indicates that the null is rejected at 5 percent.

experience no takeover activity and firms that experience some type of takeover activity. In panel B, the coefficients describe the relationship between the ownership structure of firms that experience no management turnover and the ownership structure of firms that experience some management turnover.

In panel A, estimates from the constrained model are not suggestive of a relationship between ownership and takeover activity. But the F-test of the hypothesis $\beta_1 = \beta_2 = \beta_3$ (in the unconstrained model) rejects the null at 1 percent for four of seven ownership variables. In two other cases, the test statistic rejects at 5 percent. These results, as well as the estimates from the unconstrained model, indicate that imposing the constraint $\beta_1 = \beta_2 = \beta_3$ obfuscates the relationship between ownership and takeover activity, which varies systematically with the status of takeover defense.

Two patterns are apparent in the estimates from the unconstrained model. First, there are significant differences in ownership between firms that are taken over and firms that are not taken over. Second, within the group of firms that are not taken over, the ownership structure of firms that have no takeover defenses tends to be very different than the ownership structure of firms that have poison pill defenses. The ownership structure of firms with takeover defenses other than poison pills represents an intermediate case between the two extremes.

The estimates of β_2 suggest that ownership of CEOs, other officers and directors, and institutions at firms that have poison pill defenses and experience no takeover activity is less than that observed at firms that have poison pills and are takeover targets. This contrast in ownership structure is not, however, statistically significant; none of the estimates for β_2 rejects the null at 10 percent. There is a statistically significant difference between the ownership structure of nontargets that have poison pill defenses and the ownership structure of nontargets that have no defenses; we reject at 1 percent the null hypothesis $\beta_1 = \beta_2$ for four of the seven ownership variables. We also reject $\beta_1 = \beta_2 = \beta_3$ in these same cases. These results suggest that ownership structure also may play a role in explaining the correlation between takeover defense and takeover activity.

5.4 Ownership and Management Turnover

The results in panel B of table 5.2 are qualitatively similar to those in panel A. The estimates from the constrained model reveal that the null of no relationship between management turnover and owner-ship is rejected at 5 percent for four of the seven ownership variables that we consider. The estimates suggest that insiders (CEOs, officers, and directors) with strong ownership positions are unlikely to experience turnover. Strong institutional ownership is associated with an increased likelihood of management turnover. These findings are consistent with the evidence in Denis, Denis, and Sarin (1997), Allen (1981), and Salancik and Pfeffer (1980).

Turning to the unconstrained model, we see that ownership structure varies with takeover defense among firms that do not experience management turnover. The estimates of β_1 in panel B indicate that an absence of management turnover is associated with strong insider ownership at firms that have no takeover defenses. There is a statistically significant difference between the ownership structure of no-turnover firms that have poison pill defenses and the ownership structure of no-turnover firms that have no defenses. We reject at 1 percent the null hypothesis $\beta_1 = \beta_2$ for four of the seven ownership variables. We also reject $\beta_1 = \beta_2 = \beta_3$ in these same cases.

The evidence in table 5.2 suggests that ownership, like perfor-mance, may play a role in explaining both the correlation between takeover defense and takeover activity and the correlation between takeover defense and management turnover. Moreover, the results in tables 5.1 and 5.2 suggest that the identification problem discussed in chapter 3 is an issue of genuine importance. Empirically, we see that ownership, performance, and control activity are correlated. Eco-nomic theory suggests that these characteristics of firms are jointly determined. Econometric models that ignore these relationships may yield misleading inference.

6

Probit Models

6.1 Ownership, Performance, Defensive Activity, and Takeovers

In table 6.1, we examine probit models that explain takeover activity with performance, ownership, and takeover defense. In each model, the dependent variable assumes a value of 1 if a completed takeover or buyout occurs and a value of 0 if no takeover or buyout occurs. Attempted takeovers that are not successful are classified as no takeover. A size control (total assets) is included in each model. Estimates of the coefficients associated with this variable and the constant are not reported.

Our approach is motivated by the results presented in tables 5.1 and 5.2, which reveal respectively a significant interaction between performance and takeover defense and a significant interaction between ownership and takeover defense. In table 6.1, we focus on the interaction between performance and takeover defense. Models that address the interaction between ownership and takeover defense reveal that ownership plays a secondary role to performance in explaining takeover activity. Estimation of the interaction between takeover defense and explanatory variables increases the number of explanatory variables by 2 for each interaction that we consider. If the sample size were unlimited, we would estimate a model where takeover defense interacts simultaneously with different measures of performance and all ownership variables and test the constraints associated with the hypothesis that certain variables or interactions are irrelevant. We find that for the sample considered here, large models appear to be overparameterized. For many permutations of the sample, the probit estimator will not converge.

The most general model in table 6.1 is presented in the first row and labeled model 1. All others are nested within it. In the general

Table 6.1
Performance, ownership, takeover defense, and takeover activity

Bootstrap coefficient estimates of probit models that explain takeover activity with ownership, financial performance and takeover defense.

	Ownership		Cash-Flow-Based Return on Assets[a]			Takeover Defense		Difference in Sensitivity of Takeovers to Performance[b]			Test of Joint Restrictions[c]	
	CEO Ownership β_1	Director Ownership β_2	No Defense[d] β_3	Poison Pill β_4	Other Defense[e] β_5	No Defense[d] β_6	Poison Pill β_7	$\beta_3 - \beta_4$	$\beta_3 - \beta_5$	$\beta_4 - \beta_5$	Wald	Pval
Model 1												
	1.35	-1.88	0.67	-1.72	-2.09	-0.34	-0.65	2.39	2.76	0.37		
	0.59	-1.13	0.92	-2.32	-1.08	-0.50	-0.89	2.31	1.12	0.14		
Model 2												
	1.24	-1.81	0.29	-1.66	-1.28			1.95	1.57	-0.38	0.70	0.70
	0.59	-1.15	0.62	-3.20	-1.53			4.12	1.93	-0.43		
Model 3												
	1.06	-1.54	-0.54			-0.32	0.58				0.86	0.65
	0.53	-0.96	-1.22			-0.10	1.85					
Model 4												
						0.71					0.53	1.00
						2.83						

Note: Each set of estimates is based on 400 bootstrap replications of the sample, weighted to correct for sample-selection bias. Z-statistics based on the bootstrap estimate of the parameter covariance matrix are noted below the coefficients. The dependent variable has a value of 1 if a takeover or leveraged buyout occurs and a value of zero otherwise. All models use the sample of 312 NYSE- and AMEX-listed firms for which complete financial data are available. The test period is 1984 through 1987. Estimated coefficients are labeled $\beta_0, \ldots, \beta_8$, where β_0 corresponds to the constant and β_8 corresponds to the size control.

Table 6.1
(*continued*)

a. The explanatory variables are interactive. Cash flow is multiplied by a dummy that represents the status of takeover defenses at the firm in question. The takeover defense categories are defined in notes d and e. β_3, β_4, and β_5 are the coefficients associated with no defense, poison pill, and other defense, respectively.

b. Performance is measured as the prior four years of cash-flow-based return on assets. The test statistics, which represent variation in the sensitivity of takeover activity to performance as a function of takeover defense, have an asymptotic distribution that is unit normal. They are calculated with the bootstrap.

c. The Wald statistic for model 2 is a test of the hypothese $\beta_6 = \beta_7 = 0$. The null hypothesis is that the probability of takeover activity is independent of the presence of takeover defense. The Wald statistic for model 3 is a test of the hypothesis that $\beta_3 = \beta_4 = \beta_5$. The null hypothesis is that the relationship between performance and takeover activity is independent of the presence of takeover defense. Both statistics have an asymptotic distribution that is $\chi^2(2)$. The Wald statistic for model 4 is a test of the hypothesis that $\beta_1 = \beta_2 = \beta_3 = \beta_4 = \beta_5 = \beta_7 = \beta_8 = 0$. The null hypothesis is that the cross-sectional variation in takeover activity is explained by takeover defense alone. This has an asymptotic distribution that is $\chi^2(7)$. All Wald statistics are calculated using the bootstrap estimate of the robust covariance matrix from model 1. The calculation of the test statistic is described in White (1982).

d. Firms that did not have a fair-price provision, classified board amendment, or poison pill.

e. Firms that had a fair-price provision or classified board amendment but no poison pill.

† Indicates that a test statistic rejects the null at 1 percent.

‡ Indicates that a test statistic rejects the null at 5 percent.

model, takeover defense influences takeover activity both directly and through performance. We test this model against an alternative where takeover defense has no direct impact on the likelihood of a takeover (model 2), an alternative where the relationship between takeover activity and performance is independent of takeover defense (model 3), and an alternative where only takeover defense affects the likelihood of a takeover (model 4). Evidence concerning the validity of these restrictions is provided by a set of Wald statistics and a battery of z-tests. An analysis of the sampling distribution of the Wald statistic demonstrates that it has low power in the setting considered here. For this reason, we rely mainly on the more powerful z-statistics for inference. A rejection of the null implies that the general model provides a better description of the data than does the restricted model.

Models 1 and 2 in table 6.1 acknowledge the possibility that the relationship between takeover activity and financial performance depends on the status of takeover defense. (This is a maintained hypothesis.) Model 2 is a constrained version of model 1, where takeover defense does not directly influence the likelihood of a takeover. The z-statistics associated with no defense (β_6) and poison pill (β_7) in model 1 are a test of this constraint, as is the Wald statistic associated with the second model. We also test the maintained hypothesis that the relationship between takeover activity and performance is independent of takeover defense, using the z-statistics labeled $\beta_3 - \beta_4$, and so on.

The estimates from these models indicate that the apparent influence of takeover defense on takeover activity is in fact attributable to the interaction between performance and takeover defense, as noted in table 5.1. In table 6.1, estimates from the first two models reveal a negative correlation between performance and takeover activity at firms that have takeover defenses; the relationship is statistically significant at firms that have poison pills. No variable other than performance has statistically significant explanatory power. In particular, there is no evidence of a direct relationship between takeover activity and takeover defense; neither the z-statistic associated with no defense nor the z-statistic associated with poison pill rejects the null. We do reject the hypothesis that the relationship between performance and takeover activity at firms without takeover defenses is the same as the relationship between performance and takeover activity at firms with poison pills. This suggests that the maintained hypothesis in models 1 and 2 is an important feature of the data.

The results in model 1 are consistent with the findings in Ambrose and Megginson (1992), Song and Walkling (1993), and Mikkelson and Partch (1989). Similar to our results, Ambrose and Megginson find a negative, though statistically insignificant, relationship between poison pills and takeovers and between antitakeover charter amendments and takeovers. Song and Walkling (1993) and Mikkelson and Partch (1989) find a statistically significant negative relationship between director ownership and the probability of being a takeover target. We also document a negative, though statistically somewhat less significant, relationship between director ownership and takeover probability. Unlike the earlier studies, our standard errors are based on the bootstrap estimate of the parameter covariance matrix.

In model 3, we constrain the relationship between performance and takeover activity to be independent of type of takeover defense. Imposition of this constraint, which is rejected by the data, produces an estimate that suggests that poison pills *increase* the likelihood of a takeover. In other words, the introduction of a performance variable reverses the relationship between takeover defense and takeover activity.

In model 4, we ignore the influence of all variables other than takeover defense. Estimates from this model suggest that takeover defense decreases the frequency of takeover activity. But the z-statistics associated with models 1 and 2 indicate that the restriction that sustains this inference is inconsistent with the data. In short, the evidence in table 6.1 suggests that performance and little else explains the frequency of takeover activity and that this relationship exists only at firms that have takeover defenses.

We find that these conclusions are insensitive to whether LBOs are included in the sample; if they are deleted, the dependent variable has a value of 1 only in those cases where control shifts to an outsider. If stock-market returns or growth in cash-flow-based ROA are used as performance measures, the relationship between performance and takeover activity becomes statistically insignificant. But in no case do we observe evidence of a direct relationship between takeover defense and takeover activity. Moreover, a nonnested likelihood ratio test suggested by Vuong (1989) rejects models based on stock-market performance or cash-flow growth as alternatives to the model described in the first row of table 6.1.

Our interpretation of this evidence reflects our concern about identification. We suspect that the absence of correlation between performance and takeover activity at firms that have no takeover defense is attributable to some characteristic of these firms other than the status of takeover defenses. The relationship between ownership and takeover defense documented in table 5.2 is suggestive, but we are unable to establish a link. We nonetheless discuss the hypothesis that attributes the evidence presented in table 6.1 to self-selection.

Suppose that certain firms seek business combinations for strategic reasons that are unrelated to performance. Those firms would have little incentive to adopt takeover defenses. Then in the data, we would observe no correlation between performance and takeover activity at these firms. We would also observe a negative cross-sectional correlation between defensive activity and takeover activity. But that correlation would be attributable to the fact that firms without takeover defenses seek to be taken over rather than to any causal relationship based on performance or the efficacy of takeover defense.

We also note that while the relationship between performance and takeover activity at firms that have takeover defenses (poison pills) indicates that takeover defenses are not 100 percent effective, this result does not imply that defensive activity is completely ineffective. Nor does it imply that the adoption of takeover defenses is costless. There are a number of cases in our sample where it seems clear that poor performance attributable to inept management persisted for long periods of time, at least partly because of defensive activity. This is consistent with evidence from announcement returns as noted by Bhagat and Jefferis (1991) and Ryngaert (1988).

Our analysis also suggests how one might go about measuring the impact of takeover defense on the link between performance and takeover activity. If substandard cash flow leads to takeovers, and defensive activity attenuates this link, then the probability of a takeover given poor cash flow should be reduced by the presence of takeover defense. This implies that the duration of poor performance should, on average, be extended by the presence of takeover defense. The evidence presented here indicates that an investigation along these lines should control for self-selection, perhaps through the use of panel data.

6.2 Ownership, Performance, Defensive Activity, and Managerial Turnover

Probit models that explain management turnover with performance, ownership, and takeover defense are presented in table 6.2. In each model, the dependent variable assumes a value of 1 if some management turnover occurs and a value of 0 if no management turnover occurs. We make no distinction between partial turnover and complete turnover. A size control (total assets) is included in each model. Estimates of the coefficients associated with this variable and the constant are not reported. The structure of the econometric model is identical to the structure of the model presented in table 6.1, save for the fact that cash-flow growth rather than cash flow is used to measure performance.

Our results concerning management turnover are qualitatively similar to the results concerning takeover activity presented above. We observe a statistically significant relationship between management turnover and performance but only at firms that have poison pills. Our estimates indicate that at these institutions, poor performance is associated with the subsequent departure of the CEO. The data provide no evidence of direct relationship between takeover defense and management turnover, as would be suggested by the hypothesis that managers who enjoy the protection of takeover defenses are "entrenched." The hypothesis that the relationship between management turnover and performance is independent of takeover defense is rejected by the data. If we nevertheless impose this constraint, the estimates indicate that poor performance is associated with management turnover.

We find that these results are not sensitive to the definition of turnover or performance. Our estimates have substantially the same properties as the estimates reported in table 6.2 if we delete from the sample either observations associated with complete management turnover or observations associated with partial management turnover. The use of stock-market return rather than cash-flow growth as a performance measure does not alter our conclusions. Some specifications of the econometric model yield estimates that are not statistically significant. No specification produces evidence that takeover defense is an effective means for managers to retain their positions, independent of performance.

Table 6.2
Performance, ownership, takeover defense, and management turnover

Bootstrap coefficient estimates of probit models that explain management turnover with performance, ownership, and takeover defense.

	Ownership		Growth in Cash-Flow-Based Return on Assets[a]			Takeover Defense		Difference in Sensitivity of Turnover to Performance[b]			Test of Joint Restrictions	
	CEO Ownership β_1	Director Ownership β_2	No Defense[c] β_3	Poison Pill β_4	Other Defense[d] β_5	No Defense β_6	Poison Pill β_7	$\beta_3 - \beta_4$	$\beta_3 - \beta_5$	$\beta_4 - \beta_5$	Wald[e]	pval
Model 1												
	−0.61	−1.35	−0.14	−5.28	−0.21	−0.13	0.14	5.15	0.07	−5.07		
	−0.48	−1.47	−0.09	−3.05	−0.07	−0.55	0.50	2.18	0.02	−1.41		
Model 2												
	−0.52	−1.10	−0.31	−4.85	−0.41			4.54	0.10	−4.43	0.07	0.97
	−0.41	−1.24	−0.21	−2.93	−0.16			2.04	0.04	−1.42		
Model 3												
	−0.38	−1.28	−1.90			0.00	0.16				0.19	0.91
	−0.29	−1.36	−1.79			0.01	0.61					
Model 4												
						−0.03					0.02	1.00
						−0.16						

Note: Each set of estimates is based on 400 bootstrap replications of the sample, weighted to correct for sample-selection bias. Z-statistics based on the bootstrap estimate of the parameter covariance matrix are noted below the coefficients. The dependent variable has a value of 1 if the firm experiences either complete management turnover or partial management turnover and a value of zero otherwise. All models use the sample of 312 NYSE- and AMEX-listed firms for which the necessary financial data are available. The test period is 1984 through 1987. Estimated coefficients are labeled $\beta_0, \ldots, \beta_8$, where β_0 corresponds to the constant and β_8 corresponds to the size control.

Table 6.2
(*continued*)

a. The explanatory variables are interactive. Cash-flow growth is multiplied by a dummy that represents the status of takeover defenses at the firm in question. The takeover defense categories are defined in notes c and d. β_3, β_4, and β_5 are the coefficients associated with no defense, poison pill, and other defense, respectively.

b. Performance is measured as the prior four years' growth in cash-flow-based return on assets. The test statistics, which are calculated using bootstrap estimates of the standard errors, have an asymptotic distribution that is unit normal. The parameters of the model are $\beta_0, \ldots, \beta_8$, where β_0 corresponds to the constant and β_8 corresponds to the size control.

c. Firms that did not have a fair-price provision, classified board amendment, or poison pill.

d. Firms that had a fair-price provision or classified board amendment but no poison pill.

e. The Wald statistic for model 2 is a test of the hypothesis $\beta_6 = \beta_7 = 0$. The null hypothesis is that the probability of takeover activity is independent of the presence of takeover defense. The Wald statistic for model 3 is a test of the hypothesis that $\beta_3 = \beta_4 = \beta_5$. The null hypothesis is that the relationship between performance and takeover activity is independent of the presence of takeover defense. Both statistics have an asymptotic distribution that is $\chi^2(2)$. The Wald statistic for model 4 is a test of the hypothesis that $\beta_1 = \beta_2 = \beta_3 = \beta_4 = \beta_5 = \beta_7 = \beta_8 = 0$. The null hypothesis is that the cross-sectional variation in takeover activity is explained by takeover defense alone. This has an asymptotic distribution that is $\chi^2(7)$. All Wald statistics are calculated using the bootstrap estimate of the robust covariance matrix from the most general model, which appears in the first row of the table. The calculation of the test statistic is described in White (1982).

6.3 Diagnostics

We construct a battery of diagnostic statistics for the probit models. The focus of this effort is the detection of heteroscedasticity. Our tests include graphical analysis of the psuedo-residuals as described by Pagan and Vella (1989), the conditional moment test developed by Newey (1985), and a Hausman test based on the difference between the (normalized) probit estimates and score estimates. Evidence reported by Skeels and Vella (1999) indicates that the conditional moment test is not very powerful in the case of the probit estimator, although Newey has shown that the test has optimal asymptotic power locally. A Monte Carlo study confirms that this test has low power for our data as well. This observation motivates our Hausman test.

Hausman tests are based on the difference between two estimators. One is consistent and efficient under the null hypothesis that the model is correctly specified. A second is consistent under both the null and the alternative but inefficient under the null. In the case considered here, the probit estimator is consistent and efficient under the maintained assumption that the latent error terms in equation 2.1 have a homoscedastic normal distribution but inconsistent if this assumption is violated. The score estimator β^* is consistent but inefficient if the latent errors are well behaved and consistent if the maintained assumptions of the probit model are violated. If Σ is the covariance matrix for these two estimators, the Hausman test statistic is

$$H = (\beta - \beta^*)\Sigma^{-1}(\beta - \beta^*). \qquad (6.1)$$

The test statistic has an asymptotic distribution that is $\chi^2(q)$, where q is the dimension of the parameter vector, under conditions discussed in White (1982). The score estimator does not satisfy those conditions, so we have no formal justification for our test. We construct an estimate of the covariance matrix Σ using bootstrap estimates from the score and probit estimators. Simulation results indicate that this test statistic is more powerful than the conditional moment test of Newey (1985) in detecting heterosedasticity. It has an empirical distribution that approaches χ^2 and would therefore appear to be an appropriate diagnostic.

Table 6.3 presents specification diagnostics for the probit models that appear in the first row of tables 6.1 and 6.2. Hausman statistics,

Table 6.3
Takeover activity and management turnover

Specification diagnostics for probit models that explain takeover activity with performance, ownership, and takeover defense and probit models that explain management turnover with performance, ownership, and takeover defense.

Panel A: Takeover activity[a]

Estimator	Ownership		Cash-Flow-Based Return on Assets[b]			Takeover Defense		Conditional Moment Tests[c]		Hausman Test[d]
	CEO Ownership	Director Ownership	No Defense	Poison Pill	Other Defense	No Defense	Poison Pill	Normality	Heteroscedasticity	H
Probit	0.20	-0.20	-0.59	0.12	-0.23	-0.15	-0.22	1.12	2.13	19.77†
Score	0.24	-0.13	-0.38	0.20	-0.08	-0.19	-0.27			
Hausman[e]	0.54	-1.43	-19.56†	0.08	10.97†	0.01	0.03			

Panel B: Management turnover[f]

Estimator	Ownership		Growth in Cash-Flow-Based Return on Assets			Takeover Defense		Conditional Moment Tests		Hausman Test
	CEO Ownership	Director Ownership	No Defense	Poison Pill	Other Defense	No Defense	Poison Pill	Normality	Heteroscedasticity	H
Probit	-0.11	-0.23	0.26	-0.01	-0.73	0.01	0.05	.49	1.78	5.93
Score	-0.10	-0.17	0.30	0.00	-0.48	0.03	0.08			
Hausman	0.17	2.68†	5.69†	0.54	51.91†	0.02	0.04			

Note: Each set of estimates is based on 400 bootstrap replications of the sample, weighted to correct for sample-selection bias. For each permutation of the sample, we compute a probit estimate, which is then normalized to have unit length, and a score estimate, which has unit length by construction. The norm is a nonlinear operator.

Table 6.3
(continued)

a. The dependent variable has a value of 1 if a takeover or leveraged buyout occurs and a value of zero otherwise. The score estimator and probit estimator both use permutations of the sample of 312 observations for which the necessary financial data are available.

b. The explanatory variables are interactive. Cash flow is multiplied by a dummy that represents the status of takeover defenses at the firm in question. The category of no defense is composed of firms that do not have a fair-price provision, classified board amendment, or poison pill. The category of other defense is composed of firms that have a fair-price provision or classified board amendment but no poison pill. Estimated coefficients are labeled $\beta_1, \ldots, \beta_8$, where β_1 corresponds to CEO ownership and β_8 corresponds to the size control. β_3, β_4, and β_5 are the coefficients associated with no defense, poison pill, and other defense, respectively.

c. Conditional moment tests for normality and heteroscedasticity are developed in Newey (1985) and discussed in Skeels and Vella (1999). Skeels and Vella find that these tests have low power in the probit model. A Monte Carlo experiment documented in appendix G* confirms that this is also the case for the data reported here. The conditional moment test has an asymptotic χ^2 distribution under the null hypothesis.

d. Our Hausman (1978) test is based on the sampling distribution for the score estimator and probit estimator. We construct the covariance matrix for the two estimators under the null using a Monte Carlo procedure that is described in appendix H*. The omnibus statistic has an asymptotic distribution that is $\chi^2(8)$ under the null hypothesis of consistent estimation.

e. The test statistic has a unit normal distribution under the null hypothesis of consistent estimation.

f. The dependent variable has a value of 1 if the firm experiences either complete management turnover or partial management turnover and 0 otherwise. All models use the sample of 292 observations for which the necessary financial data are available.

† Indicates that the test statistic rejects the null at 1 percent.

* Indicates that the test statistic rejects the null at 1 percent.

* Appendixes G and H are available at ⟨http://leeds.colorado.edu/faculty/bhagat⟩.

which are based on the difference between the probit estimator and the score estimator, are presented along with the score estimates and probit estimates that are used to construct the Hausman test. Score estimates have unit length. (This is a property of the estimator.) The probit estimates have been normalized to facilitate comparison. Hausman statistics for the individual coefficients are reported on a coefficient by coefficient basis. The omnibus Hausman statistic for the model appears in the right-hand column of the table. We also present conditional moment tests for normality and heteroscedasticity. In both panel A, which concerns the model of takeover activity presented in table 6.1, and panel B, which concerns the model of management turnover from table 6.2, the correspondence between the probit estimates and the score estimates is generally close. The Hausman test nonetheless rejects the null of consistent estimation for the coefficients associated with other defense and no defense in both models. In the model of management turnover, the Hausman test also suggests that the coefficient associated with ownership by officers and directors is not estimated consistently. The omnibus statistic rejects the null for the model of takeover activity but not the model of management turnover. We conclude that the parameter estimates in tables 6.1 and 6.2 should be interpreted with caution.

The conditional moment tests for normality and heteroscedasticity fail to reject the null. Our Monte Carlo study of these tests indicates that the test statistics have very low power in the setting considered here. For this reason, we regard the failure of these statistics to reject the null as uninformative.

7   Summary and Conclusions

A vast theoretical and empirical literature in corporate finance considers the interrelationships between corporate governance, takeovers, management turnover, corporate performance, corporate capital structure, and corporate ownership structure. Most of the extant literature considers the relationship between two of these variables at a time—for example, the relationship between ownership and performance or the relationship between corporate governance and takeovers.

The following is just a sampling from the above-mentioned literature: Pound (1987) and Comment and Schwert (1995) consider the effect of takeover defenses on takeover activity; Morck, Shleifer, and Vishny (1989) examine the effect of corporate ownership and firm performance on takeover activity and management turnover; De-Angelo and DeAngelo (1989), Martin and McConnell (1991), Denis and Serrano (1996), and Mikkelson and Partch (1997) consider the effect of firm performance on management turnover; Denis, Denis, and Sarin (1997) consider the effect of ownership structure on management turnover; Bhagat and Jefferis (1991) consider the impact of corporate ownership structure on takeover defenses; Ikenberry and Lakonishok (1993) investigate the effect of firm performance on takeover activity; Berkovitch, Israel, and Spiegel (1998) examine the impact of capital structure on management compensation; Mahrt-Smith (2000) studies the relationship between ownership and capital structure; Garvey and Hanka (1999) investigate the impact of corporate governance on capital structure; McConnell and Servaes (1990), Hermalin and Weisbach (1991), Loderer and Martin (1997), Cho (1998), Himmelberg, Hubbard, and Palia (1999), Aggarwal and Samwick (2001), and Demsetz and Villalonga (2001) study the relationship between managerial ownership and firm performance; and

DeAngelo and DeAngelo (2000) and Fenn and Liang (2001) focus on ownership structure and the corporate payout policy.

We argue that takeover defenses, takeovers, management turnover, corporate performance, capital structure, and corporate ownership structure are interrelated. Hence, from an econometric viewpoint, the proper way to study the relationship between any two of these variables would be to set up a system of simultaneous equations that specifies the relationships between these six variables. However, specification and estimation of such a system of simultaneous equations is nontrivial.

For example, econometric models that acknowledge the possibility that performance, ownership, and takeover defenses influence takeovers do not necessarily yield consistent estimates for the parameters of interest. Identification requires some combination of exclusion restrictions, assumptions about the joint distribution of the error terms, and restrictions on the functional form of the structural equations. Maddala (1983) discusses restrictions that identify the model when the error terms are normally distributed. Identification in *single-equation* semiparametric index models, where the functional form is unknown and the explanatory variables in that equation are continuous, known functions of a basic parameter vector, is discussed by Ichimura and Lee (1991). Estimation of a system of equations in the absence of strong restrictions on *both* the functional form of the equations and the joint distribution of error terms is, to the best of our knowledge, an unsolved problem.

We are unaware of a model of takeover defense that implies specific functional forms. If these functions are linear, identification may be attained through either strong distributional assumptions or exclusion restrictions. Maddala (1983) and Amemiya (1985) discuss restrictions on the error terms that identify the model in the absence of exclusion restrictions. But these restrictions are inconsistent with incentive-based explanations of takeover defense, since unobservable characteristics of managerial behavior or type will be reflected in all of the error terms. Exclusion restrictions are therefore the most likely path to identification.

The hypothesis that we wish to test—that takeover defense affects the likelihood of takeover activity—suggests that exclusion restrictions would be difficult to justify. Intuitively, variables that affect the likelihood of a takeover will be reflected in the structure of takeover defenses.

To illustrate this problem in a meaningful manner, we consider the following two questions that have received considerable attention in the literature and have significant policy implications: do antitakeover measures prevent takeovers, and do antitakeover measures help managers enhance their job tenure?

We examine the impact of firm performance, ownership structure, and corporate takeover defenses on takeover activity and managerial turnover. Our focus is the efficacy of corporate takeover defense. The literature suggests that takeovers and the managerial labor market serve to discipline poor performers in the managerial ranks and also suggests that corporate takeover defenses are designed to shield incumbent managers from these forces. If this is in fact the case, and the belief that motivates the adoption of takeover defenses is rational, the presence of these defenses should be associated with a decline in takeover activity and extended job tenure for managers. The results presented here provide little support for this hypothesis. We do observe a negative correlation between takeover activity and takeover defense that is statistically significant. But the introduction of a performance variable into a model that relates takeover activity to takeover defense reverses the sign of the relationship between takeover activity and takeover defense. In a model that allows the relationship between performance and takeover activity to vary with takeover defense, we find that defensive activity is ineffective. This ineffectiveness of takeover defenses is consistent with the findings of Comment and Schwert (1995).

Our specification test suggests that we "ask too much of the data" when we fit the probit model that attempts to explain takeovers (or turnovers) as a function of corporate ownership structure, corporate performance, and takeover defenses. We also have a concern about identification of such probit models. However, our evidence does suggest that performance and ownership structure may play an important role in explaining the frequency of takeover activity. These variables should not be omitted from investigations of this phenomenon.

In the case of management turnover, our results are even stronger. The frequency of CEO departures is uncorrelated with the status of takeover defenses at firms in our sample. This statement is consistent with both simple correlations and with the estimates from probit models, where we find that turnover is related to performance. At firms with poison pill defenses, there is a statistically significant relationship between management turnover and performance.

We stress that these results do not imply that defensive activity is costless to shareholders. It may well be the case that managers who are shielded by takeover defenses perform less well than they would have had the takeover defenses not been in place. This hypothesis is consistent with both the results reported here and with indirect evidence from announcement returns. Our evidence does, however, suggest quite strongly that takeover defenses are not completely effective in insulating managers from the consequences of poor performance.

Appendix: Sensitivity Analysis

The tables in this appendix are numbered in a manner that corresponds to the tables in chapters 5 and 6. For example, sensitivity analyses related to table 5.1 are labeled table 5.1.A, table 5.1.B, and so on. The substance of the sensitivity analysis is described in the table captions and is summarized here.

Table 5.1. Performance versus takeover activity and management turnover.
Table 5.1.A includes a size control in the regression.
Table 5.1.B varies the definitions of takeover activity and management turnover.

Table 5.2. Ownership versus takeover activity and management turnover.
Table 5.2.A includes a size control in the regression.

Table 6.1. Performance, ownership, takeover defense, and takeover activity.
Table 6.1.A varies the definition of takeover activity.

Table 6.2. Performance, ownership, takeover defense, and management turnover.
Table 6.2.A. Performance measure is stock return during the 200 trading days preceding the proxy mailing.
Table 6.2.B varies the definition of management turnover.
Table 6.2.C varies the definition of management turnover again.
Table 6.2.D sets weights to 1:1.

Table 5.1.A
Sensitivity analysis: Performance versus takeover activity and management turnover (includes a size control)

Estimated coefficients and t-statistics from bootstrap regressions of performance measures on dummy variables that represent the joint experience of firms with respect to takeover activity and takeover defense and the joint experience of firms with respect to management turnover and takeover defense. A size control is included in all regressions but not reported.

Panel A: Performance versus takeover activity

Performance Measure	Nobs	Interactive Dummy for No Takeover Activity and Takeover Defense[a]				Test[b] $\beta_1 = \beta_2$	Test[c] $\beta_1 = \beta_2 = \beta_3$	Dummy for No Takeover Activity	
		Const	No Defense	Poison Pill	Other Defense			Const	Dummy[d]
Market-adjusted stock returns for 200 trading days preceding test period	303	-2.75	8.16	22.45	2.40	2.19	2.54	-2.62	16.24
		-0.29	0.59	2.10	0.15			-0.28	1.59
Cash-flow-based return on assets, years -4 through -1	312	46.26	4.50	9.82	8.10	2.95	2.04	46.25	8.56
		10.52	0.76	3.00	1.62			10.51	2.69
Growth in cash-flow-based return on assets, years -4 through -1	312	-2.50	-1.79	0.27	-0.94	3.71	2.48	-2.51	-0.33
		-2.46	-0.55	0.25	-0.60			-2.46	-0.29

Panel B: Performance versus management turnover

Performance Measure	Nobs	Interactive Dummy for No Management Turnover and Takeover Defense[e]				Test $\beta_1 = \beta_2$	Test $\beta_1 = \beta_2 = \beta_3$	Dummy for No Management Turnover	
		Const	No Defense	Poison Pill	Other Defense			Const	Dummy
Market-adjusted stock returns for 200 trading days preceding test period	303	2.58	-11.14	35.00	5.31	8.68†	5.16†	3.14	18.15
		0.44	-0.74	3.26	0.36			0.54	1.96

Table 5.1.A
(*continued*)

	N							N		
Cash-flow-based return on assets, years −4 through −1	312	51.32	3.54	5.93	1.64	1.03	1.13	312	51.35	4.54
		12.53	0.69	1.61	0.31				12.54	1.50
Growth in cash-flow-based return on assets, years −4 through −1		−3.56	1.84	2.83	0.73	1.37	1.50		−3.55	2.20
		−3.99	0.74	2.47	0.38				−3.97	1.95

Note: Each set of estimates is based on 200 bootstrap replications of the sample, weighted to correct for sample-selection bias. The number of observations varies because of missing financial data.

a. Dummy variables have a value of 1 if the firm experiences no takeover activity and has the specified type of takeover defense. The takeover defense categories are mutually exclusive and collectively exhaustive. A positive coefficient indicates that firms that experience no takeover activity and have the specified type of takeover defense exhibit positive performance relative to the set of firms that experience some type of takeover activity. The omitted category is firms that experience either an attempted takeover or a completed takeover. The performance of this group is represented by the intercept term.

b. The test statistic is distributed $F(1, N - 4)$. See Amemiya (1985).

c. The test statistic is distributed $F(2, N - 4)$. See Amemiya (1985).

d. The t-statistic in the constrained regression is a test of the null hypothesis $\beta_1 = \beta_2 = \beta_3 = 0$ against the alternative $\beta_1 = \beta_2 = \beta_3 = k \neq 0$.

e. Dummy variables have a value of 1 if the firm experiences no management turnover and has the specified type of takeover defense. The takeover defense categories are mutually exclusive and collectively exhaustive. A positive slope coefficient indicates that firms that experience no management turnover and have the specified type of takeover defense exhibit positive performance relative to the set of firms that experience some management turnover. The omitted category is firms that experience either partial management turnover or complete management turnover. The performance of this group is captured in the intercept term.

† Indicates that the null hypothesis is rejected at 1 percent.

‡ Indicates that the null hypothesis is rejected at 5 percent.

Table 5.1.B
Sensitivity analysis: Performance versus takeover activity and management turnover (with definitions varied)

Estimated coefficients and t-statistics from bootstrap regressions of performance measures on dummy variables that represent the joint experience of firms with respect to takeover activity and takeover defense, and the joint experience of firms with respect to management turnover and takeover defense. The definitions of no takeover activity and no management turnover are changed.

Panel A: Performance versus takeover activity

Performance Measure	Nobs	Interactive Dummy for No Takeover Activity and Takeover Defense[a]				Test[b] $\beta_1 = \beta_2$	Test[c] $\beta_1 = \beta_2 = \beta_3$	Dummy for No Takeover Activity	
		Const	No Defense	Poison Pill	Other Defense			Const	Dummy[d]
Market-adjusted stock returns for 200 trading days preceding test period	303	3.59 0.30	−0.59 −0.04	13.70 1.07	−12.78 −0.75	2.27	3.68[†]	3.59 0.30	6.45 0.51
Cash-flow-based return on assets, years −4 through −1	312	47.79 8.53	1.81 0.30	7.18 1.53	3.34 0.57	2.50	2.14	47.79 8.53	5.59 1.21
Growth in cash-flow-based return on assets, years −4 through −1	312	−1.53 −1.04	−2.75 −0.86	−0.41 −0.27	−1.48 −0.78	4.03[‡]	2.60	−1.53 −1.04	−0.98 −0.65

Panel B: Performance versus management turnover

Performance Measure	Nobs	Interactive Dummy for No Management Turnover and Takeover Defense[e]				Test $\beta_1 = \beta_2$	Test $\beta_1 = \beta_2 = \beta_3$	Dummy for No Management Turnover	
		Const	No Defense	Poison Pill	Other Defense			Const	Dummy
Market-adjusted stock returns for 200 trading days preceding test period	303	2.03 0.15	1.53 0.09	16.39 1.12	−16.96 −0.92	2.49	5.13[†]	2.03 0.15	7.92 0.56

Table 5.1.B
(*continued*)

Cash-flow-based return on assets, years −4 through −1	312	45.78	6.98	9.08	3.85	1.49	1.96	45.78	7.77
		7.24	0.98	1.62	0.62			7.24	1.39
Growth in cash-flow-based return on assets, years −4 through −1	312	−2.02	−1.32	−0.14	−0.67	3.33	2.23	−2.02	−0.43
		−1.67	−0.39	−0.10	−0.41			−1.67	−0.31

Note: Each set of estimates is based on 200 bootstrap replications of the sample, weighted to correct for sample-selection bias. The number of observations varies because of missing financial data.

a. Dummy variables have a value of 1 if the firm experiences either no takeover activity or an attempted takeover that is unsuccessful and has the specified type of takeover defense. The takeover defense categories are mutually exclusive and collectively exhaustive. A positive slope coefficient indicates that firms that experience either no takeover activity or an unsuccessful attempt and have the specified type of takeover defense exhibit performance in excess of that observed at firms that experience a completed takeover by either insiders or outsiders. The omitted category is firms that experience a completed takeover. Mean performance for this group is represented by the intercept term.

b. The test statistic is distributed $F(1, N-4)$. See Amemiya (1985).

c. The test statistic is distributed $F(2, N-4)$. See Amemiya (1985).

d. The t-statistic in the constrained regression is a test of the null hypothesis $\beta_1 = \beta_2 = \beta_3 = 0$ against the alternative $\beta_1 = \beta_2 = \beta_3 = k \neq 0$.

e. Dummy variables have a value of 1 if the firm experiences either no management turnover or partial management turnover and has the specified type of takeover defense. The takeover defense categories are mutually exclusive and collectively exhaustive. A positive slope coefficient indicates that firms that experience either no management turnover or partial management turnover and have the specified type of takeover defense exhibit performance in excess of that observed at firms that experience complete management turnover. The omitted category is firms that experience complete management turnover. Mean performance for this group is represented by the intercept term.

† Indicates that the null hypothesis is rejected at 1 percent.

‡ Indicates that the null hypothesis is rejected at 5 percent.

Table 5.2.A
Sensitivity analysis: Ownership versus takeover activity and management turnover (includes a size control)

Estimated coefficients and t-statistics from bootstrap regressions of ownership on dummy variables that represent the joint experience of firms with respect to takeover activity and the joint experience of firms with respect to management turnover and takeover defense. A size control is included but not reported.

Panel A: Ownership versus takeover activity

Ownership	Interactive Dummies for No Takeover Activity and Takeover Defense[a]						Dummy for No Takeover Activity	
	Const	No Defense	Poison Pill	Other Defense	Test[b] $\beta_1 = \beta_2$	Test[c] $\beta_1 = \beta_2 = \beta_3$	Const	Dummy[d]
Chief executive officer	5.15	5.05	-2.52	1.29	24.57[†]	13.82[‡]	5.13	-0.45
	3.30	1.86	-1.64	0.62			3.30	-0.29
Directors and officers	11.50	8.64	-3.52	3.30	30.70[†]	17.69[‡]	11.46	-0.08
	5.58	2.76	-1.78	1.19			5.56	-0.04
Institutions	41.26	-13.60	0.67	-11.46	25.11[†]	17.83[‡]	41.35	-4.09
	11.42	-3.98	0.26	-3.53			11.42	-1.70
Block ownership by officers	6.38	9.73	-1.96	2.41	32.30[†]	16.94[‡]	6.36	0.98
	3.36	2.79	-0.98	0.99			3.36	0.50
Block ownership by directors	2.99	-0.11	-2.06	-1.22	5.01[‡]	3.02	2.99	-1.56
	2.54	-0.06	-1.70	-0.81			2.54	-1.27
Block ownership by institutions	3.16	-0.07	-0.83	-0.80	2.30	1.57	3.16	-0.69
	4.89	-0.06	-1.24	-0.90			4.89	-1.02
Block ownership by ESOPs	1.89	-1.66	-0.09	-0.52	5.03[‡]	2.81	1.89	-0.46
	3.67	-3.13	-0.16	-0.83			3.67	-0.84

Panel B: Ownership versus management turnover

Ownership	Interactive Dummies for No Management Turnover and Takeover Defense						Dummy for No Management Turnover	
	Const	No Defense	Poison Pill	Other Defense	Test $\beta_1 = \beta_2$	Test $\beta_1 = \beta_2 = \beta_3$	Const	Dummy
Chief executive officer	3.79	9.42	0.08	2.48	21.34†	11.23†	3.73	2.68
	4.77	2.68	0.07	1.35			4.68	2.11
Directors and officers	9.67	16.35	0.12	4.98	31.70†	16.51†	9.55	4.73
	8.28	3.75	0.09	1.58			8.24	2.89
Institutions	41.20	−14.90	−4.12	−12.59	8.44†	5.60†	41.31	−8.25
	12.78	−3.49	−1.54	−3.96			12.78	−3.58
Block ownership by officers	5.79	15.65	−0.11	2.10	34.09†	17.78†	5.69	3.86
	5.87	3.16	−0.07	1.09			5.80	2.32
Block ownership by directors	2.06	0.20	−1.18	0.19	2.10	1.77	2.05	−0.58
	3.77	0.12	−1.74	0.15			3.76	−0.82
Block ownership by institutions	2.85	−0.97	−0.26	−1.45	1.78	1.48	2.86	−0.67
	6.82	−0.89	−0.31	−2.43			6.86	−1.13
Block ownership by ESOPs	1.44	−0.49	0.31	0.43	1.55	1.29	1.45	0.16
	4.20	−0.66	0.54	0.59			4.18	0.37

Note: Each set of estimates is based on 200 bootstrap replications of the sample, weighted to correct for sample-selection bias. All regressions use the full sample of 344 observations.

a. Dummy variables have a value of 1 if the firm experiences no takeover activity and has the specified type of takeover defense. The takeover defense categories are mutually exclusive and collectively exhaustive. A positive slope coefficient indicates that firms that experience no takeover activity and have the specified type of takeover defense exhibit ownership in excess of that observed at firms that experience some type of takeover activity. The omitted category is firms that experience either an attempted takeover or a completed takeover. Mean ownership for this group is represented by the intercept term.

b. The test statistic is distributed as F(1,340) under the null $\beta_1 = \beta_2$.

c. The test statistic is distributed as F(2,340) under the null $\beta_1 = \beta_2 = \beta_3$.

d. The t-statistic is a test of the null hypothesis $\beta_1 = \beta_2 = \beta_3 = 0$ against the alternative $\beta_1 = \beta_2 = \beta_3 = k \neq 0$.

† Indicates that the null is rejected at 1 percent.

‡ Indicates that this same hypothesis rejected at 5 percent.

Table 6.1.A
Sensitivity analysis: Performance, ownership, takeover defense, and takeover activity (with definitions varied)

Bootstrap estimates of probit models that represent the influence of performance, ownership, and takeover defense on takeover activity. Estimated coefficients and z-statistics are based on 400 bootstrap replications of the sample. The definition of the dependent variable is changed.

Panel A

Dependent variable has a value of 1 if the firm experiences a completed takeover or leveraged buyout and a value of 0 otherwise. The sample consists of 312 firms for which cash-flow information is available.

CEO Ownership	Director Ownership	Cash-Flow-Based Return on Assets					Difference in Sensitivity of Takeovers to Performance[a]			Wald[b]
		No Defense	Pill	Other Defense	No Defense	Pill	$\beta_3 - \beta_4$	$\beta_3 - \beta_5$	$\beta_4 - \beta_5$	
1.35	−1.88	0.67	−1.72	−2.09	−0.34	−0.65	2.39	2.76	0.37	
0.59	−1.13	0.92	−2.32	−1.08	−0.50	−0.89	2.31	1.12	0.14	
1.24	−1.81	0.29	−1.66	−1.28			1.95	1.57	−0.38	0.70
0.59	−1.15	0.62	−3.20	−1.53			4.12	1.93	−0.43	
1.06	−1.54	−0.54			−0.32	0.58				0.86
0.53	−0.96	−1.22			−0.10	1.85				

Panel B

Dependent variable has a value of 1 if the firm experiences a completed takeover and a value of 0 otherwise. Leveraged buyouts are deleted from the sample. The sample consists of 302 firms for which cash-flow information is available.

CEO Ownership	Director Ownership	Cash-Flow-Based Return on Assets					Difference in Sensitivity of Takeovers to Performance[a]			Wald[b]
		No Defense	Pill	Other Defense	No Defense	Pill	$\beta_3 - \beta_4$	$\beta_3 - \beta_5$	$\beta_4 - \beta_5$	
1.25	−1.15	0.89	−2.20	−2.94	−0.63	−1.20	3.09	3.83	0.74	
0.50	−0.71	1.11	−2.26	−1.29	−0.80	−1.45	2.15	1.12	0.30	

Table 6.1.A
(*continued*)

1.08	−1.06	0.18	−2.12	−1.40			2.30	1.58	−0.72	1.33
0.48	−0.71	0.37	−3.33	−1.63			3.69	2.03	−0.82	
0.89	−0.72	−0.58			−0.53	0.45				0.87
0.43	−0.47	−1.27			−1.65	1.35				

Panel C

Dependent variable has a value of 1 if the firm experiences a completed takeover and a value of 0 otherwise. The sample consists of 312 firms for which cash-flow information is available.

CEO Ownership	Institutional Ownership	Cash-Flow-Based Return on Assets					Difference in Sensitivity of Takeovers to Performance[a]			
		No Defense	Pill	Other Defense	No Defense	Pill	$\beta_3 - \beta_4$	$\beta_3 - \beta_5$	$\beta_4 - \beta_5$	Wald
−0.09	0.83	0.37	−1.78	−2.23	−0.31	−0.50	2.15	2.60	0.45	
−0.05	1.22	0.50	−2.35	−0.78	−0.39	−0.68	2.12	1.35	0.22	
−0.01	0.87	0.09	−1.79	−1.47			1.88	1.56	−0.32	0.45
−0.01	1.34	0.21	−3.21	−1.58			3.77	1.63	−0.42	
0.12	1.00	−0.72			−0.30	0.62				0.82
0.08	1.53	−1.65			−0.93	1.88				

a. The test statistics, which are calculated using bootstrap estimates of the standard errors, have an asymptotic distribution that is unit normal.
b. The first Wald statistic is a test of the hypothesis that $\beta_3 = \beta_4 = \beta_5$. The null hypothesis is that the relationship between performance and takeover activity is indepenent of the presence of takeover defense. The second Wald statistic is a test of the hypothesis $\beta_6 = \beta_7 = 0$. The null hypothesis is that the probability of takeover activity is independent of the presence of takeover defense. Both statistics have an asymptotic distribution that is $\chi^2(2)$. The statistics are calculated using the bootstrap estimates of the parameters and their covariance matrix. Monte Carlo simulations indicate that the finite sample distribution of the test statistic differs significantly from its asymptotic distribution and also indicate that both statistics have very low power.

Table 6.2.A
Sensitivity analysis: Performance, ownership, takeover defense, and management turnover (with performance measure defined)

Bootstrap estimates of probit models that represent the influence of performance, ownership, and takeover defense on management turnover. Performance measure is market-adjusted stock return over the 200 trading days preceding the estimation period.

CEO Owner-ship	Director Owner-ship	Market-Adjusted Stock Return					Difference in Sensitivity of Turnover to Performance[a]			Test of Joint Restrictions	
		No Defense	Pill	Other Defense	No Defense	Pill	$\beta_3 - \beta_4$	$\beta_3 - \beta_5$	$\beta_4 - \beta_5$	Wald[b]	pval
−0.61	−1.35	−0.14	−5.28	−0.21	−0.13	0.14	5.15	0.07	−5.07		
−0.48	−1.47	−0.09	−3.05	−0.07	−0.55	0.50	2.18	0.02	−1.41	0.60	0.74
−0.52	−1.10	−0.31	−4.85	−0.41			4.54	0.10	−4.43		
−0.41	−1.24	−0.21	−2.93	−0.16			2.04	0.04	−1.42	0.19	0.91
−0.38	−1.28	−1.90			0.00	0.16					
−0.29	−1.36	−1.79			0.01	0.61				0.02	1.00
		−0.03									
		−0.16									

Note: Estimated coefficients and z-statistics are based on 400 bootstrap replications of the sample. Dependent variable has a value of 1 if the firm experiences any type of management turnover and a value of 0 otherwise. The sample consists of 303 firms for which all financial data are available.

a. The test statistics, which are calculated using bootstrap estimates of the standard errors, have an asymptotic distribution that is unit normal. The parameters of the model are $\beta_0, \ldots, \beta_8$, where β_0 corresponds to the constant and β_8 corresponds to the size control.

b. The first Wald statistic is a test of the hypothesis $\beta_6 = \beta_7 = 0$. The null hypothesis is that the probability of takeover activity is independent of the presence of takeover defense. The second Wald statistic is a test of the hypothesis that $\beta_3 = \beta_4 = \beta_5$. The null hypothesis is that the relationship between performance and takeover activity is independent of the presence of takeover defense. Both statistics have an asymptotic distribution that is $\chi^2(2)$. The third Wald statistic is a test of the hypothesis that $\beta_1 = \beta_2 = \beta_3 = \beta_4 = \beta_5 = \beta_7 = \beta_8 = 0$. The null hypothesis is that the cross-sectional variation in takeover activity is explained by takeover defense alone. This has an asymptotic distribution that is $\chi^2(7)$. All Wald statistics are calculated using the bootstrap estimate of the robust covariance matrix from the most general model, which appears in the first row of the table. The calculation of the test statistic is described in White (1982).

Table 6.2.B
Sensitivity analysis: Performance, ownership, takeover defense, and management turnover (with definitions varied)

Bootstrap estimates of probit models that represent the influence of performance, ownership, and takeover defense on management turnover. The dependent variable has a value of 1 if management turnover is complete and a value of zero if there is no management turnover. Observations associated with partial management turnover are deleted from the sample.

CEO Owner-ship	Director Owner-ship	Growth in Cash-Flow-Based Return on Assets					Difference in Sensitivity of Turnover to Performance[a]			Test of Joint Restrictions	
		No Defense	Pill	Other Defense	No Defense	Pill	$\beta_3 - \beta_4$	$\beta_3 - \beta_5$	$\beta_4 - \beta_5$	Wald[b]	pval
-0.38	-1.47	-0.16	-5.71	0.83	-0.26	0.09	5.56	-0.99	-6.54	0.93	0.63
-0.30	-1.61	-0.09	-3.47	0.26	-1.06	0.33	2.38	-0.27	-1.82		
-0.27	-1.13	-0.36	-5.04	0.30			4.68	-0.66	-5.34	0.87	0.65
-0.22	-1.24	-0.23	-3.17	0.10			2.21	-0.20	-1.63		
-0.16	-1.40	-1.78			-0.08	0.14				1.19	0.98
-0.12	-1.47	-1.53			-0.37	0.55					
0.01		0.01									
0.06		0.06									

Note: Estimated coefficients and z-statistics are based on 400 bootstrap replications of the sample. The dependent variable has a value of 1 if the firm experiences any type of management turnover and a value of 0 otherwise. The sample consists of 312 firms for which all financial data are available.

a. The test statistics, which are calculated using bootstrap estimates of the standard errors, have an asymptotic distribution that is unit normal. The parameters of the model are $\beta_0, \ldots, \beta_8$, where β_0 corresponds to the constant and β_8 corresponds to the size control.

b. The first Wald statistic is a test of the hypothesis $\beta_6 = \beta_7 = 0$. The null hypothesis is that the probability of takeover activity is independent of the presence of takeover defense. The second Wald statistic is a test of the hypothesis that $\beta_3 = \beta_4 = \beta_5$. The null hypothesis is that the relationship between performance and takeover activity is independent of the presence of takeover defense. Both statistics have an asymptotic distribution that is $\chi^2(2)$. The third Wald statistic is a test of the hypothesis that $\beta_1 = \beta_2 = \beta_3 = \beta_4 = \beta_5 = \beta_7 = \beta_8 = 0$. The null hypothesis is that the cross-sectional variation in takeover activity is explained by takeover defense alone. This has an asymptotic distribution that is $\chi^2(7)$. All Wald statistics are calculated using the bootstrap estimate of the robust covariance matrix from the most general model, which appears in the first row of the table. The calculation of the test statistic is described in White (1982).

Table 6.2.C
Sensitivity analysis: Performance, ownership, takeover defense, and management turnover (with definitions varied again)

Bootstrap estimates of probit models that represent the influence of performance, ownership, and takeover defense on management turnover. The dependent variable has a value of 1 if management turnover is partial and a value of zero if there is no management turnover. Observations associated with complete management turnover are deleted from the sample.

CEO Owner-ship	Director Owner-ship	Growth in Cash-Flow-Based Return on Assets					Difference in Sensitivity of Turnover to Performance[a]			Test of Joint Restrictions	
		No Defense	Pill	Other Defense	No Defense	Pill	$\beta_3 - \beta_4$	$\beta_3 - \beta_5$	$\beta_4 - \beta_5$	Wald[b]	pval
-0.63	-1.37	0.19	-5.04	-0.40	-0.21	0.11	5.23	0.59	-4.64	0.81	0.67
-0.50	-1.47	0.13	-2.85	-0.13	-0.90	0.38	2.26	0.19	-1.34		
-0.51	-1.07	-0.05	-4.46	-0.85			4.40	0.80	-3.61	0.84	0.66
-0.41	-1.18	-0.04	-2.65	-0.32			2.01	0.28	-1.16		
-0.40	-1.29	-1.63			-0.08	0.11					
-0.31	-1.33	-1.53			-0.40	0.42					
		-0.02									
		-0.10									

Note: Estimated coefficients and z-statistics are based on 400 bootstrap replications of the sample. The dependent variable has a value of 1 if the firm experiences any type of management turnover and a value of 0 otherwise. The sample consists of 312 firms for which all financial data are available.

a. The test statistics, which are calculated using bootstrap estimates of the standard errors, have an asymptotic distribution that is unit normal. The parameters of the model are $\beta_0, \ldots, \beta_8$, where β_0 corresponds to the constant and β_8 corresponds to the size control.

b. The first Wald statistic is a test of the hypothesis $\beta_6 = \beta_7 = 0$. The null hypothesis is that the probability of takeover activity is independent of the presence of takeover defense. The second Wald statistic is a test of the hypothesis that $\beta_3 = \beta_4 = \beta_5$. The null hypothesis is that the relationship between performance and takeover activity is independent of the presence of takeover defense. Both statistics have an asymptotic distribution that is $\chi^2(2)$. The third Wald statistic is a test of the hypothesis that $\beta_1 = \beta_2 = \beta_3 = \beta_4 = \beta_5 = \beta_7 = \beta_8 = 0$. The null hypothesis is that the cross-sectional variation in takeover activity is explained by takeover defense alone. This has an asymptotic distribution that is $\chi^2(7)$. All Wald statistics are calculated using the bootstrap estimate of the robust covariance matrix from the most general model, which appears in the first row of the table. The calculation of the test statistic is described in White (1982).

Table 6.2.D
Sensitivity analysis: Performance, ownership, takeover defense, and management turnover (with weights set to 1:1)

Bootstrap estimates of probit models that represent the influence of performance, ownership, and takeover defense on management turnover. The estimation procedure does not involve weighting to correct for sample-selection bias.

CEO Owner-ship	Director Owner-ship	Growth in Cash-Flow-Based Return on Assets					Difference in Sensitivity of Turnover to Performance[a]			Test of Joint Restrictions	
		No Defense	Pill	Other Defense	No Defense	Pill	$\beta_3 - \beta_4$	$\beta_3 - \beta_5$	$\beta_4 - \beta_5$	Wald[b]	pval
-0.61	-1.39	-0.00	-5.24	0.27	-0.17	0.07	5.24	-0.28	-5.52		
-0.43	-1.45	-0.00	-3.11	0.08	-0.66	0.22	2.21	-0.07	-1.50		
-0.52	-1.17	-0.19	-4.81	-0.12			4.62	-0.07	-4.69	0.64	0.73
-0.36	-1.25	-0.12	-3.00	-0.04			2.10	-0.02	-1.49		
-0.33	-1.33	-1.77			-0.01	0.10				0.85	0.65
-0.23	-1.36	-1.58			-0.07	0.39					
		-0.07								1.07	0.98
		-0.37									

Note: Estimated coefficients and z-statistics are based on 400 bootstrap replications of the sample. Dependent variable has a value of 1 if the firm experiences any type of management turnover and a value of 0 otherwise. The sample consists of 312 firms for which all financial data are available.

a. The test statistics, which are calculated using bootstrap estimates of the standard errors, have an asymptotic distribution that is unit normal. The parameters of the model are $\beta_0, \ldots, \beta_8$, where β_0 corresponds to the constant and β_8 corresponds to the size control.

b. The first Wald statistic is a test of the hypothesis $\beta_6 = \beta_7 = 0$. The null hypothesis is that the probability of takeover activity is independent of the presence of takeover defense. The second Wald statistic is a test of the hypothesis that $\beta_3 = \beta_4 = \beta_5$. The null hypothesis is that the relationship between performance and takeover activity is independent of the presence of takeover defense. Both statistics have an asymptotic distribution that is $\chi^2(2)$. The third Wald statistic is a test of the hypothesis that $\beta_1 = \beta_2 = \beta_3 = \beta_4 = \beta_5 = \beta_7 = \beta_8 = 0$. The null hypothesis is that the cross-sectional variation in takeover activity is explained by takeover defense alone. This has an asymptotic distribution that is $\chi^2(7)$. All Wald statistics are calculated using the bootstrap estimate of the robust covariance matrix from the most general model, which appears in the first row of the table. The calculation of the test statistic is described in White (1982).

References

Aggarwal, Rajesh K., and Andrew A. Samwick. 2001. Empire-builders and shirkers: Investment, firm performance, and managerial incentives. Working paper, Dartmouth College.

Agrawal, Anup, and Charles R. Knoeber. 1996. Firm performance and mechanisms to control agency problems between managers and shareholders. *Journal of Financial and Quantitative Analysis* 31: 377–397.

Agrawal, Anup, and Charles R. Knoeber. 1999. Outside directors, politics, and firm performance. Working paper, Social Science Research Network Electronic Library, available at http://papers.ssrn.com/papers.taf?abstract_id=125348.

Allen, Michael P. 1981. Managerial power and tenure in the large corporation. *Social Forces* 60: 482–494.

Ambrose, Brent W., and William L. Megginson. 1992. The role of asset structure, ownership structure, and takeover defenses in determining acquisition likelihood. *Journal of Financial and Quantitative Analysis* 27: 575–590.

Amemiya, Takeshi. 1985. *Advanced econometrics*. Cambridge, MA: Harvard University Press.

American Law Institute. 1994. *Principles of corporate governance*. Philadelphia: ALI.

Barber, Brad M., and John D. Lyon. 1996. Detecting abnormal operating performance: The empirical power and specification of test statistics. *Journal of Financial Economics* 41: 359–400.

Barber, Brad, and John Lyon. 1997. Detecting long-run abnormal stock returns: The empirical power and specification of test statistics. *Journal of Financial Economics* 43: 341–372.

Barclay, Michael J., and Clifford G. Holderness. 1992. The law and large-block trades. *Journal of Law and Economics* 35: 265–294.

Barnhart, Scott W., and Stuart Rosenstein. 1998. Board composition, managerial ownership, and firm performance: An empirical analysis. *Financial Review* 33: 1–16.

Baysinger, Barry, and Henry Butler. 1985. Corporate governance and the board of directors: Performance effects of changes in board composition. *Journal of Law, Economics and Organization* 1: 101–124.

Bebchuk, Lucian Arye, and Lars A. Stole. 1993. Do short-term objectives lead to under- or overinvestment in long-term projects? *Journal of Finance* 48: 719–729.

Berger, Philip G., Eli Ofek, and David L. Yermack. 1997. Managerial entrenchment and capital structure decisions. *Journal of Finance* 52: 1411–1438.

Berkovitch, Elazar, Ronen Israel, and Yossef Spiegel. 1998. Managerial compensation and capital structure. Working paper, University of Michigan.

Berle, A. A., Jr., and G. C. Means. 1932. *The modern corporation and private property.* New York: MacMillan.

Bethel, Jennifer E., Julia Porter Liebeskind, and Tim Opler. 1998. Block share purchases and corporate performance. *Journal of Finance* 53: 605–634.

Bhagat, Sanjai, and Bernard Black. 2001. Board independence and long-term firm performance. *Journal of Corporation Law* 27.

Bhagat, Sanjai, Bernard Black, and Margaret Blair. 2001. Relational investing and firm performance. Working paper, Stanford University.

Bhagat, Sanjai, Denis Carey, and Charles Elson. 1999. Director ownership, corporate performance, and management turnover. *The Business Lawyer* 54: 885–919.

Bhagat, Sanjai, and Jefferis, Richard H. 1991. Voting power in the proxy process: The case of antitakeover charter amendments. *Journal of Financial Economics* 30: 193–225.

Bhagat, Sanjai, Andrei Shleifer, and Robert W. Vishny. 1990. Hostile takeovers in the 1980s: The return to corporate specialization. *Brookings Papers on Economic Activity: Microeconomics* (1990): 1–84.

Bhagat, Sanjai, and Jefferis, Richard H. 1994. The causes and consequences of takeover defense: Evidence from greenmail. *Journal of Corporate Finance* 1: 201–231.

Bishop, Y., S. E. Feinberg, and P. W. Holland. 1976. *Discrete multivariate analysis.* Cambridge, MA: MIT Press.

Black, Bernard. 1990. Shareholder passivity reexamined. *Michigan Law Review* 89: 520–608.

Black, Bernard. 1992a. Agents watching agents: The promise of institutional investor voice. *UCLA Law Review* 39: 811–893.

Black, Bernard. 1992b. The value of institutional investor monitoring: The empirical evidence. *UCLA Law Review* 39: 895–939.

Black, Bernard. 1998. Shareholder activism and corporate governance in the United States. *The new Palgrave dictionary of economics and the law* (vol. 3, pp. 459–465). New York: W. W. Norton.

Black, Bernard, and John C. Coffee, Jr. 1994. Hail Britannia? Institutional investor behavior under limited regulation. *Michigan Law Review* 92: 1997–2087.

Brickley, James A., Ronald C. Lease, and Clifford Smith. 1988. Ownership structure and voting on antitakeover amendments. *Journal of Financial Economics* 20: 267–291.

Bruner, Robert F. 1991. *The poison pill anti-takeover defense: The price of strategic deterrence.* Charlottesville, VA: Institute of Chartered Financial Analysts.

Byrd, John W., and Kent A. Hickman. 1992. Do outside directors monitor managers? Evidence from tender offer bids. *Journal of Financial Economics* 32: 195–222.

California Public Employees Retirement System. 1998. *Corporate governance core principles and guidelines.* Sacramento, CA, available at http://www.calpers-governance.org/principles/domestic/us/page01.asp.

Carleton, William T., James M. Nelson, and Michael S. Weisbach. 1998. The influence of institutions on corporate governance through private negotiations: Evidence from TIAA-CREF. *Journal of Finance* 53: 1335–1362.

Cho, Myeong-Hyeon. 1998. Ownership structure, investment, and the corporate value: An empirical analysis. *Journal of Financial Economics* 47: 103–121.

Comment, Robert, and G. William Schwert. 1995. Poison or placebo? Evidence on the deterrence and wealth effects of modern antitakeover measures. *Journal of Financial Economics* 39: 3–43.

Comment, Robert, and G. William Schwert. 1997. Hostility in takeovers: In the eyes of the beholder. Working paper, University of Rochester.

Core, John E., Robert W. Holthausen, and David F. Larcker. 1999. Corporate governance, chief executive officer compensation, and firm performance. *Journal of Financial Economics* 51: 371–406.

Cosslett, S. 1981. Maximum likelihood estimator for choice-based samples. *Econometrica* 49: 1289–1316.

Council of Institutional Investors. 1998. *Shareholder bill of rights.* Washington, DC: CII.

Danielson, Morris, and Jonathan Karpoff. 1998. On the uses of corporate governance provisions. *Journal of Corporate Finance* 4: 347–371.

DeAngelo, Harry, and Linda DeAngelo. 1989. Proxy contests and the governance of publicly held corporations. *Journal of Financial Economics* 23: 29–60.

DeAngelo, Harry, and Linda DeAngelo. 2000. Controlling stockholders and the disciplinary role of corporate payout policy: A study of the Times Mirror Company. *Journal of Financial Economics* 56: 153–208.

DeAngelo, Harry, and Edward M. Rice. 1983. Antitakeover charter amendments and stockholder wealth. *Journal of Financial Economics* 11: 329–360.

Demsetz, Harold. 1983. The structure of ownership and the theory of the firm. *Journal of Law and Economics* 26: 375–390.

Demsetz, Harold, and Belen Villalonga. 2001. Ownership structure and corporate performance. Working paper, UCLA.

Denis, David J., and Diane K. Denis. 1995. Performance changes following top management dismissals. *Journal of Finance* 50: 1029–1058.

Denis, David J., Diane K. Denis, and Atulya Sarin. 1997. Ownership structure and top executive turnover. *Journal of Financial Economics* 45: 193–221.

Denis, David J., and Atulya Sarin. 1999. Ownership and board structures in publicly traded corporations. *Journal of Financial Economics* 52: 187–223.

Denis, David J., and Jan M. Serrano. 1996. Active investors and management turnover following unsuccessful control contests. *Journal of Financial Economics* 40: 239–266.

Efron, B. 1979. Bootstrap methods: Another look at the jackknife. *Annals of Statistics* 7: 1–26.

Fama, Eugene F. 1980. Agency problems and the theory of the firm. *Journal of Political Economy* 88: 288–307.

Fenn, George W., and Nellie Liang. 2001. Corporate payout policy and managerial stock incentives. *Journal of Financial Economics* 60: 45–72.

Fershtman, C., and K. Judd. 1987. Equilibrium incentives in oligopoly. *American Economic Review* 77: 927–940.

Fisch, Jill. 1994. Relationship investing: Will it happen? Will it work? *Ohio State Law Journal* 55: 1009–1048.

Fleming, Michael. 1993. Large-stake investors and corporate performance. Manuscript, Harvard University.

Garvey, Gerald T., and Gordon Hanka. 1999. Capital structure and corporate control: The effect of antitakeover statutes on firm leverage. *Journal of Finance* 54: 519–546.

Gordon, Lilli, and John Pound. 1992. Active investing in the U.S. equity market: Past performance and future prospects. Report prepared for the California Public Employees' Retirement System, Sacramento.

Griliches, Zvi, and Jacques Mairesse. 1999. Production functions: The search for identification. Working paper, Harvard University.

Grossman, Sanford, and Oliver Hart. 1983. An analysis of the principal-agent problem. *Econometrica* 51: 7–45.

Grossman, Sanford, and Oliver Hart. 1986. The costs and benefits of ownership: A theory of vertical and lateral integration. *Journal of Political Economy* 44: 691–719.

Harris, Milton, and Artur Raviv. 1988. Corporate control contests and capital structure. *Journal of Financial Economics* 20: 55–86.

Harris, Milton, and Artur Raviv. 1991. The theory of capital structure. *Journal of Finance* 46: 297–355.

Harris, Milton, and Artur Raviv. 1992. Financial contracting theory. In *Advances in Economic Theory*. Cambridge: Cambridge University Press.

Hart, Oliver, and John Moore. 1990. Property rights and the theory of the firm. *Journal of Political Economy* 48: 1119–1158.

Hausman, Jerry. 1978. Specification tests in econometrics. *Econometrica* 46: 1251–1272.

Hermalin, Benjamin E., and Michael S. Weisbach. 1988. The determinants of board composition. *Rand Journal of Economics* 19: 589–606.

Hermalin, Benjamin E., and Michael S. Weisbach. 1991. The effect of board composition and direct incentives on firm performance. *Financial Management* 21: 101–112.

Himmelberg, Charles P., R. Glenn Hubbard, and Darius Palia. 1999. Understanding the determinants of Managerial ownership and the link between ownership and performance. *Journal of Financial Economics* 53: 353–384.

Holderness, Clifford, and Dennis P. Sheehan. 1985. Raiders or saviors? The evidence on six controversial investors. *Journal of Financial Economics* 14: 555–579.

Ichimura, H., and L. Lee. 1991. Semiparametric least squares estimation of multiple index models: Single-equation estimation. In W. Barnett, J. Powell, and G. Tauchen, eds., *Nonparametric and semiparametric methods in economics and statistics*. Cambridge: Cambridge University Press.

Ikenberry, David, and Josef Lakonishok. 1993. Corporate governance through the proxy context: Evidence and implications. *Journal of Business* 66: 405–435.

Investor Responsibility Research Center. 1987. *Corporate Governance Bulletin* 1. Washington, DC.

Jacobs, Michael. 1991. *Short-term America*. Boston: Harvard Business School Press.

Jarrell, Gregg A., James A. Brickley, and Jeffrey M. Netter. 1988. The market for corporate control: The empirical evidence since 1980. *Journal of Economic Perspectives* 2: 49–68.

Jarrell, Gregg A., and Annette B. Poulsen. 1987. Shark repellents and stock prices: The effects of antitakeover amendments since 1980. *Journal of Financial Economics* 19: 127–168.

Jensen, Michael C. 1986. Agency costs of free cash flow, corporate finance, and takeovers. *American Economic Review* 76: 323–329.

Jensen, Michael C., and William H. Meckling. 1976. Theory of the firm: Managerial behavior, agency costs, and capital structure. *Journal of Financial Economics* 3: 305–360.

Jensen, Michael C., and Kevin J. Murphy. 1990. Performance pay and top management incentives. *Journal of Political Economy* 98: 225–264.

Jensen, Michael C., and Jerold B. Warner. 1988. The distribution of power among corporate managers, shareholders, and directors. *Journal of Financial Economics* 20: 3–24.

Karpoff, Jonathan M., and Paul H. Malatesta. 1989. The wealth effects of second-generation state takeover legislation. *Journal of Financial Economics* 25: 291–322.

Kidder, Peabody & Co. 1984. *Effects of adoption of fair price amendments on stock prices and institutional ownership*. New York: Kidder, Peabody.

Kleiman, Robert T., Kevin Nathan, and Joel M. Shulman. 1994. Are there payoffs for "patient" corporate investors? *Mergers and Acquisitions*: 34–41.

Klein, April. 1998. Firm performance and board committee structure. *Journal of Law and Economics* 41: 275–303.

Knoeber, Charles R. 1986. Golden parachutes, shark repellents, and hostile tender offers. *American Economic Review* 76: 155–167.

Kothari, S. P., and Jerold Warner. 1997. Measuring long-horizon security price performance. *Journal of Financial Economics* 43: 301–340.

Linn, Scott C., and John J. McConnell. 1983. An empirical investigation of antitakeover amendments on common stock prices. *Journal of Financial Economics* 11: 361–399.

Loderer, Claudio, and Kenneth Martin. 1997. Executive stock ownership and performance: Tracking faint traces. *Journal of Financial Economics* 45: 223–256.

Longstreth, Bevis. 1994. Corporate governance: There's danger in new orthodoxies. *Corporate Governance Advisor*: 18–21.

Lowenstein, Louis. 1991. *Sense and nonsense in corporate finance.* Reading, MA: Addison-Wesley.

Lyon, John, Brad Barber, and Chih Tsai. 1999. Improved methods for tests of long-run abnormal stock returns. *Journal of Finance* 54: 165–201.

MacAvoy, Paul W., S. Cantor, J. Dana, and S. Peck. 1983. ALI proposals for increased control of the corporation by the board of directors: An economic analysis. In *Statement of the business roundtable on the American Law Institute's proposed "Principles of corporate governance and structure: Restatement and recommendations."* New Haven, CT: ALI.

Maddala, G. S. 1983. *Limited-dependent and qualitative variables in econometrics.* New York: Cambridge University Press.

Mahrt-Smith, Jan. 2000. The interaction of capital structure and ownership dispersion. Working paper, London Business School.

Manski, Charles F. 1975. Maximum score estimation of the stochastic utility model of choice. *Journal of Econometrics* 3(3): 205–228.

Manski, Charles, and S. Lerman. 1977. The estimation of choice probabilities from choice-based samples. *Econometrica* 45: 1977–1988.

Manski, Charles, and D. McFadden. 1981. Alternative estimators and sample designs for discrete choice analysis. In C. F. Manski and D. McFadden, eds., *Structural analysis of discrete data with econometric applications.* Cambridge, MA: MIT Press.

Manski, Charles, and S. Thompson. 1986. Operational characteristics of maximum score estimation. *Journal of Econometrics* 32: 85–108.

Martin, Kenneth J., and John J. McConnell. 1991. Corporate performance, corporate takeovers, and management turnover. *Journal of Finance* 46: 671–688.

McConnell, John, and Henri Servaes. 1990. Additional evidence on equity ownership and corporate value. *Journal of Financial Economics* 27: 595.

McEachern, William. 1975. *Managerial control and performance.* Lexington, MA: Lexington Books.

McFadden, Daniel. 1989. A method of simulated moments for estimation of discrete response models without numerical integration. *Econometrica* 57: 995–1026.

Mikhail, W. M. 1975. A comparative Monte Carlo study of the properties of econometric estimators. *Journal of the American Statistical Association* 70: 94–104.

Mikkelson, Wayne H., and Megan M. Partch. 1989. Managers' voting rights and corporate control. *Journal of Financial Economics* 25: 263–290.

Mikkelson, Wayne H., and Megan M. Partch. 1997. The decline of takeovers and disciplinary managerial turnover. *Journal of Financial Economics* 44: 205–228.

Mikkelson, Wayne H., and Richard S. Ruback. 1985. An empirical analysis of the interfirm equity investment process. *Journal of Financial Economics* 14: 523–553.

Millstein, Ira. 1993. The evolution of the certifying board. *Business Lawyer* 48: 1485–1497.

Morck, Randolph, Andrei Shleifer, and Robert Vishny. 1988. Management ownership and market valuation: An empirical analysis. *Journal of Financial Economics* 20: 293–316.

Morck, Randolph, Andrei Shleifer, and Robert Vishny. 1989. Alternative mechanisms for corporate control. *American Economic Review* 79: 842–852.

Murphy, Kevin J., and Jerold L. Zimmerman. 1993. Financial performance surrounding CEO turnover. *Journal of Accounting and Economics* 16: 273–316.

Myerson, Roger. 1987. Incentive compatibility and the bargaining problem. *Econometrica* 47: 61–73.

National Association of Corporate Directors. 1996. *Report of the NACD blue ribbon commission on director professionalism*. Washington, DC: NACD.

Newey, Whitney. 1985. Maximum likelihood specification testing and conditional moment tests. *Econometrica* 53: 1047–1070.

Novaes, Walter, and Luigi Zingales. 1999. Capital structure choice under a takeover threat. Working paper, University of Chicago.

Pagan, A., and F. Vella. 1989. Diagnostic tests for models based on individual data: A survey. *Journal of Applied Econometrics* 4: S29–S59.

Pakes, Ariel, and David Pollard. 1989. Simulation and asymptotics of optimization estimators. *Econometrica* 57: 1027–1058.

Palepu, Krishna G. 1986. Predicting takeover targets: A methodological and empirical analysis. *Journal of Accounting and Economics* 8: 3–36.

Porter, Michael. 1992. Capital choices: Changing the way America invests. In *Industry research report presented to the Council on Competitiveness*. Boston: Harvard Business School Press.

Pound, John. 1987. The effect of antitakeover amendments on takeover activity: Some direct evidence. *Journal of Law and Economics* 30: 353–368.

Roe, Mark J. 1994. *Strong managers, weak owners: The political roots of American corporate finance*. Princeton, NJ: Princeton University Press.

Romano, Roberta. 1993. Public pension fund activism in corporate governance reconsidered. *Columbia Law Review* 93: 795–853.

Rosenstein, Stuart, and Jeffrey G. Wyatt. 1990. Outside directors, board independence, and shareholder wealth. *Journal of Financial Economics* 26: 175–191.

Rosenstein, Stuart, and Jeffrey G. Wyatt. 1997. Inside directors, board effectiveness, and shareholder wealth. *Journal of Financial Economics* 44: 229–250.

Ryngaert, Michael. 1988. The effect of poison pill securities on shareholder wealth. *Journal of Financial Economics* 20: 377–418.

Salancik, Gerald R., and Jeffrey Pfeffer. 1980. Effects of ownership and performance on executive tenure in U.S. corporations. *Academy of Management Journal* 23: 653–664.

Seyhun, Nejat. 1998. *Investment intelligence from insider trading.* Cambridge, MA: MIT Press.

Shleifer, Andrei, and Robert Vishny. 1990. Equilibrium short horizons of investors and firms. *American Economic Review* 80: 148.

Skeels, C., and F. Vella. 1999. A Monte Carlo investigation of the sampling behavior of conditional moment tests in Tobit and probit models. *Journal of Econometrics* 92: 275–294.

Song, Moon H., and Ralph A. Walkling. 1993. The impact of managerial ownership on acquisition attempts and target shareholder wealth. *Journal of Financial and Quantitative Analysis* 28: 439–458.

Stein, Jeremy. 1989. Efficient capital markets, inefficient firms: A model of myopic corporate behavior. *Quarterly Journal of Economics* 104: 655–669.

Stein, Jeremy. 1996. Rational capital budgeting in an irrational world. *Journal of Business* 69: 429–455.

Stulz, Rene M. 1988. Managerial control of voting rights: Financing policies and the market for corporate control. *Journal of Financial Economics* 20: 25–54.

Theil, Henri. 1971. *Principles of econometrics.* New York: Wiley.

Vuong, Quang. 1989. Likelihood ratio tests for model selection and non-nested hypotheses. *Econometrica* 57: 307–334.

Wahal, Sunil, and John J. McConnell. 1999. Do institutional investors exacerbate managerial myopia? Working paper, Purdue University.

Wahal, Sunil, Kenneth W. Wiles, and Marc Zennner. 1995. Who opts out of state anti-takeover protection? The case of Pennsylvania's SB 1310. *Financial Management* 24: 22–39.

Warner, Jerold B., Ross L. Watts, and Karen H. Wruck. 1988. Stock prices and top management changes. *Journal of Financial Economics* 20: 461–492.

Weisbach, Michael S. 1988. Outside directors and CEO turnover. *Journal of Financial Economics* 20: 431–460.

White, Halbert. 1982. Maximum likelihood estimation of misspecified models. *Econometrica* 50: 1–25.

Yermack, David. 1996. Higher market valuation of companies with a small board of directors. *Journal of Financial Economics* 40: 185–212.

Index